MW00694539

"In *Cloud of Witnesses*, Jonathan Arnold and Zachariah Carter offer a gift to the church today from the church of the past. For two thousand years, the Spirit has worked through this great cloud of historical witnesses as they sought to contemplate God and his goodness. As we contemplate God and his goodness alongside them, that same Spirit can work in us. I pray this wonderful collection will find its way into homes, churches, and classrooms far and wide!"

Brandon D. Smith, Chair of the Hobbs School of Theology and Ministry and Associate Professor of Theology and Early Christianity, Oklahoma Baptist University; Cofounder, The Center for Baptist Renewal

"*Cloud of Witnesses* is a marvelous resource for assisting and strengthening the prayer life of Christ followers. Through the use of representative prayers from both well-known and lesser-known figures in the first nineteen centuries of the church, Jonathan Arnold and Zachariah Carter have provided readers with a well-designed and historically framed guide to refresh their communication and communion with the Trinitarian God. The modern translations and historical introductions are added benefits that greatly enhance this fine book. I am delighted to recommend *Cloud of Witnesses* and trust that it will be widely employed for both private and public use."

David S. Dockery, President, International Alliance for Christian Education

"*Cloud of Witnesses* is exactly what its title suggests: a mighty, enveloping, transcendent, and present testament to the faith from the faithful. The beauty and power of this collection is in its variety, breadth, and depth. Presented chronologically rather than topically, these prayers illuminate the history of the church and her witnesses: each individual petition occurs in a particular time and context yet affirms the eternal and universal nature of the Christian faith. This is that rare book that is both richly instructive and deeply devotional."

Karen Swallow Prior, author, *The Evangelical Imagination: How Stories, Images, and Metaphors Created a Culture in Crisis*

"I find prayer difficult, and this book is extremely helpful. If you are like me and sometimes struggle with prayer in private or with others, this book will be a great help to your personal devotions and public prayers."

Thomas White, President, Cedarville University

"Christians of any age can learn from their predecessors in the faith. Here is a range of prayers from the past that resonate with believers of the present, showing how our experience of praise, thanksgiving, confession, petition, and intercession can be enriched. The editors are historians who have supplied background information for each of the sources (nearly half of which come from the first third of the church's history) and even the original texts of the translations. Scholarship has been put at the service of today's church."

David Bebbington, Emeritus Professor of History, University of Stirling, Scotland

"With both careful scholarship and spiritual discernment, Jonathan Arnold and Zachariah Carter collect and translate significant prayers from throughout church history. As you pray with the Latin father Cyprian, the medieval theologian Bede, the Reformer Martin Luther, and the evangelical hymn writer Isaac Watts, among others, your theology will deepen and your soul will commune intimately with God. This book also includes historical commentary that explains the lives of the prayer authors and the meaning of their prayers. This is a great gift to the church of Jesus Christ that you will want to use often in both private and public worship and for theological edification."

Malcolm B. Yarnell III, Research Professor of Theology, Southwestern Baptist Theological Seminary; Teaching Pastor, Lakeside Baptist Church, Granbury, Texas; author, *Special Revelation and Scripture* and *God the Trinity*

"To be a Christian is to know God. And yet, most Christians struggle to know how to pray to God. But why should we climb this mountain alone? A great cloud of witnesses has come before us, faithful saints who show us the way up the mountain so that we can enjoy communion with our Lord. I have been looking for some time now for a single book that gives us prayers not only from the early church but also from the medieval church. At last, here it is—a treasury of prayers from the church universal. Pray them in your morning devotions. Pray them over your family. Pray them from the pulpit. And yes, pray them in the liturgy of your church. Retrieve the petitions of the ancient church, a church God has been so faithful to sustain, and do so for the sake of renewing your church today."

Matthew Barrett, Professor of Christian Theology, Midwestern Baptist Theological Seminary; Host, *Credo Podcast*; author, *Simply Trinity*

"Prayer is essential in the life of the believer. It shows our dependence on a holy and righteous God. It also affords the believer the opportunity to commune with God and worship him for who he is. But as significant as prayer is, it can be difficult to know how and what to pray. *Cloud of Witnesses* will serve as a guide for both the new and mature saint. I have prayed each prayer in this book for my family, friends, and even believers around the world. If you want communication with God that will set your heart ablaze and lead to more fruitful prayer, I commend this work to you. Have you ever struggled to pray? Oh, how you love God and know the importance of prayer. Your heart wants to pray. You make time to pray. But at the very moment you set to pray, you cannot gather the words to say. For a myriad of reasons, each of us has been in this position. If you struggle with articulating adoration, confession, thanksgiving, and petition, this book will serve as a sweet gift to you. Take these prayers and use them as a means of revival in your life and in the lives of those in your family, church, and community. God loves to answer prayer. Pray with boldness."

Kevin M. Jones, Dean of the School of Education and Social Work, Cedarville University

"Spiritual insight from spiritual giants is always powerful and rich. With so many prayers that are applicable to so many areas of one's life, *Cloud of Witnesses* is a great joy to read and to model. All believers, no matter their call in the kingdom, will benefit from this work."

Chris Osborne, Professor of Preaching, Southwestern Baptist Theological Seminary

Cloud of Witnesses

Cloud of Witnesses

A Treasury of Prayers and Petitions through the Ages

Edited by Jonathan W. Arnold
and Zachariah M. Carter

WHEATON, ILLINOIS

Cloud of Witnesses: A Treasury of Prayers and Petitions through the Ages
© 2024 by Jonathan W. Arnold and Zachariah M. Carter
Published by Crossway
        1300 Crescent Street
        Wheaton, Illinois 60187

Cover and image design: Jordan Singer

First printing 2024

Printed in China

Hardback ISBN: 978-1-4335-7058-2
ePub ISBN: 978-1-4335-7061-2
PDF ISBN: 978-1-4335-7059-9

Library of Congress Cataloging-in-Publication Data

Names: Arnold, Jonathan W. (Jonathan Wesley), 1979- editor. | Carter, Zachariah M., 1989- editor.
Title: Cloud of witnesses : a treasury of prayers and petitions through the ages / edited by
    Jonathan W. Arnold and Zachariah M. Carter.
Other titles: Cloud of witnesses (Crossway Books)
Description: Wheaton, Illinois : Crossway, 2024. | Includes bibliographical references and index.
Identifiers: LCCN 2023006936 (print) | LCCN 2023006937 (ebook) | ISBN 9781433570582
    (trade paperback) | ISBN 9781433570599 (pdf) | ISBN 9781433570612 (epub)
Subjects: LCSH: Prayers.
Classification: LCC BV245 .C543 2024 (print) | LCC BV245 (ebook) | DDC 242/.8—dc23/
    eng/20231116
LC record available at https://lccn.loc.gov/2023006936
LC ebook record available at https://lccn.loc.gov/2023006937

Crossway is a publishing ministry of Good News Publishers.

RRD			33	32	31	30	29	28	27	26	25	24
15	14	13	12	11	10	9	8	7	6	5	4	3	2	1

For my wife, Lindsay, who has taught me more about praying
in faith, hope, and love than I ever thought possible.
Jonathan

For all of the saints who petitioned heaven for my salvation.
May this be a token of a seed sown that has returned a rooted oak.
Zachariah

Contents

List of Prayers

Preface

IN ONE OF THE MOST FAMOUS and poignant passages of Scripture, Jesus's disciples recorded one of his prayers. Moved by his words, ashamed of their own anemic prayer lives, encouraged by a desire for righteousness, or some combination of these and sundry other motivations, the disciples then make a simple request—"Lord, teach us to pray" (Luke 11:1).

The book you hold in your hands is a culmination of that same request being repeated to the Lord in the intervening millennia. With the arrival of each new generation, the godly are called to pass on the faith, remind the community of saints of the goodness of God and of his actions throughout history, encourage supernatural trust in him, and help each other learn to take all requests to the God who created and sustains the universe. Prayers that have been written and published by a few of those godly followers aim to accomplish—in some small way—those goals.

Jaroslav Pelikan, the great scholar of the history of Christianity, famously said, "Tradition is the living faith of the dead, traditionalism is the dead faith of the living."[1] In many ways, this project was born from frustrations with a church experience that, in attempting to avoid what could be deemed an overreliance on tradition, lost sight of that living faith. Both of the editors of this book are Baptists who have a respect for congregational autonomy, individual faith, freedom of religion, and a healthy skepticism of human innovations in matters of the church. Unfortunately, these values have often led to a faith that has been cut off from the past. Make no mistake, we have idolized many who have come before us, but we have rarely understood their faith struggles or delved into their prayers. We have been guilty of painting the past with a broad-brush stroke that obfuscated the complexities of personal faith, and we have certainly been guilty of seeing the past in binary, black-and-white scenarios rather than struggling with both the brilliant colors and even the grays that are so often present in Scripture and in history. As historians, those weaknesses grated against every sensibility we had cultivated in our training. The realization of this weakness in our own lives

1   Jaroslav Pelikan, *The Vindication of Tradition* (New Haven: Yale University Press, 1984), 65.

created a desire to hear from the past. We longed to hear the voices of history. We longed to learn from their failures and successes. We longed to find camaraderie among the people of God. We longed to raise our voices alongside theirs, to lift our hearts in unity with them. We longed to pray with and as God's people.

Simply put, this has not always been our practice. Our small subset of the greater tradition has generally eschewed written prayers. In the early years of the Baptist community amid a fight over whether the Bible allowed for hymn singing in worship services, opponents of the practice renounced it as "a gross error equal with common national Sett forme Prayer."[2] This knee-jerk reaction certainly did not shock many involved in that particular fight. In the context of seventeenth-century England, the fear of set-form prayers made great sense. Baptist dissenters had no desire to give power to the establishment. They understood quite well the danger of having a religion only on paper, lacking both in true gospel effectiveness and godly living. They valued extemporaneous prayers that provided the listener (and speaker) with a real-time glimpse of the condition of the heart, "for out of the abundance of the heart [the] mouth speaks" (Luke 6:45).

2   Maze Pond Church Book 1 (1694–1708), Regent's Park College, Oxford.

We understand this concern, and, as good Baptists, we resonate with both the instinctive reaction and the underlying fear. But we also believe that our experience has been diminished because of our tradition's unwillingness to do the hard work of training people how to read history, including prayers from the past. We believe that using these prayers does not impair individual faith or preclude the practice of extemporaneous prayer. We believe that we can learn from the tradition—the living faith of the dead—without falling into a dead traditionalism. We pray that this is exactly what is nurtured with our book.

With this volume, we have sought to provide a broad glimpse into the faith of the church for readers of all backgrounds. The decision to include a prayer or historical figure was made based on what speaks to us and what we hope will connect with you. We have attempted to include an array of famous and lesser-known figures from the great tradition. We offer this small sample of prayers from history as an attempt to walk along this well-trodden path of faith with those who have come before us.

The original authors of these ancient prayers are not in some way more godly than other Christians. They have no unique connection to God. They are nowhere near perfect; indeed, many struggled publicly with their own besetting sins. Many even failed miserably at times in their righteous fight against those sins. Some may have made bad neighbors or contentious church members. They did not have perfect theology, nor did they get everything correct in their pastoral ministry or their personal relationships. But they all had a desire to be heard by God and to hear from him. They all pleaded the righteousness of Christ as their only right to relationship with the triune God, and they all longed for others to learn from their mistakes. They hoped that, in some small way, their congregants, colaborers, and readers would be taught to believe, pray, and depend on God—even if imperfectly.

This, then, is a book of prayers, a collection of written supplications that have been published throughout the history of the church. It is intended to be a treasure trove of insight for the reader who desires to understand the various struggles and longings of those who have already walked the path of faith. It is not intended to replace your own prayers or to improve upon the Messiah's teaching on prayer (as if it needed improvement). Rather, it is intended to encourage you to greater faith, remind you that you are not alone even in your struggles, provide a template for prayer when you are at a loss for words, and allow you to see that we are all walking this journey of faith among a great cloud of witnesses to the faithfulness of the one true God.

Prayer Books

Books of prayers such as this have been the subject of much controversy. For example, one could argue that the English Reformation itself was a contest over the Church of England's prayer book. But why? Because prayer books influence the future worship patterns of churches. During the English Reformation, one faction wanted the Book of Common Prayer—the Anglican church's book of prayer—to retain Roman Catholic influences. Another faction, the early Puritans, sought to purify those same influences in light of Scripture and regulate public worship accordingly. Thus, long before the worship wars of the late twentieth century, there was an internal struggle over the nature and content of worship among Protestants.

Our book of prayers has no ambition to supplant, direct, or order public worship. But historical debates regarding the use of prayer books do introduce our motivation for collecting, translating, modernizing, and introducing the prayers contained within this volume.

In his work on prayer, the eminent Puritan John Owen rejected the notion that written prayers must always be used in public worship, insisting that the Holy Spirit alone could animate and grant grace for believers' prayers. Owen also noted that God does not give grace to "help or assist [anyone] in composing prayers for others."[3] Thus, though Owen allowed the use of written prayers as helps for the Christian learning how to pray, he remained concerned that these written prayers not be forced on the congregation to the exclusion of impromptu prayers guided by the Spirit.

Owen found himself in the midst of heated debates about the proper form of public worship—eerie echoes of the worship wars that helped spawn the English Reformation in the previous century. He certainly did not want more written prayers to supplant the Spirit's direction, but he did want his students, congregants, and broader readership to use "any proper means" that would encourage more sincerity, higher frequency, and greater biblical faithfulness in their prayers.[4]

We agree wholeheartedly. Thus, you should think of each of the prayers in this book as both examples and templates. You should not think that reading any of these prayers automatically qualifies as praying to God with a sincere heart.

Overall, we hope that as you read these prayers you will be struck by a few things. First, we hope you will see the Trinitarian focus and structure of these prayers. Many of these prayers emphasize the inseparable work of the Father, Son, and Spirit

3 John Owen, *The Complete Works of John Owen* (Wheaton, IL: Crossway), 8:154.

4 Owen, *Works*, 8:163.

to save sinners, give mercy, and preserve the faithful. Second, we hope you will emulate their earnest supplication, or humble plea, for grace. Something that strikes us editors is the needy posture of each of these prayers. Finally, we hope you will imitate the practice of claiming God's covenant promises by faith. Not one of these figures presumed to have works-based merit that qualified them to ask for anything from God. Yet, they were confident that all promises for provision, mercy, grace, and more found their "yes" in Christ (2 Cor. 1:20).

In the preface to his own prayer book, hymnwriter Isaac Watts wondered if the stagnant religious life of Christians could be attributed to the lack of "assistance," especially in the way that most adults had seen prayer modeled when they were children.[5] While he hoped that spiritual maturity would eventually render these helps obsolete, he believed that "in such a degenerate age as this . . . all the assistance we can obtain, are little enough to uphold and promote serious Religion."[6] He hoped his prayer book would serve as a help.

We, too, long for the same thing. We commit this work to God and hope that it will be a proper aid in direction and doctrine for your own prayer life.

---

5 Issac Watts, *Prayers Composed for the Use and Imitation of Children* (London: Printed for John Clark and Richard Hett, 1728), 7.

6 Watts, *Prayers*, 7.

Editorial Changes

Each of these prayers was written in a particular historical context. That is an obvious statement, but perhaps less obvious is that each of these prayers was written to capture an individual's hopes, desires, longings, fears, and regrets. We did not want these prayers to be artificially severed from those contexts, as that would weaken the potential for these prayers to be helpful to the church. Yet, we also wanted to make them accessible to readers today.

In light of this, we have made two editorial decisions. First, we have written introductions that describe both the life and context of the author and prayer (as well as the original liturgy the prayer was published in, when applicable). We believe that knowing the historical context of the prayer will encourage your faith and garner awe for the preserving work of God.

Second, we have provided fresh translations of prayers that were not already available in English as well as modernized versions of prayers originally written in early or middle modern English. The new versions are dynamic, meaning they translate the ideas of the author rather than offer a formal word-for-word translation. Our aim has been to provide modern readings that capture the heart of the prayers. We have also added missing references for biblical quotations in brackets (but did not conform the wording of the quotation to any modern translation). Where possible, original, critical sources were translated from the Greek, Latin, and German by Jonathan, and the original text used for each new translation from these languages, as well as the original English versions, have been included in an appendix. This section will be useful to students or scholars who are interested in such historical information. All source material used for translations and modernizations is included in the historical introductions next to corresponding prayer numbers.

Additionally, we opted to remove the T-V distinction (from the Latin *tu* and *vos*) in the second-person pronouns of these prayers. In English, these forms are "thou" and "ye." The English speaker's familiarity with "thee," "thou," and "thy," among others, persisted long beyond common usage because of the prevalence of the Authorized Version in public worship. However, with the decline in common usage shortly after the publication of the 1611 Authorized Version, the prevalence of "thee" and company seems, to modern readers, to have an air of stuffiness.

Regrettably, in losing that distinction, Christians have lost a primary way of expressing their union with Christ in English. By using "thee," "thou," and "thy", the translators of the Authorized Version, the Puritans, and the eighteenth-century hymn writers were signaling a close, familial relationship with their Lord. These forms are the most ancient second-person pronouns in English, inherited from Old German. The second person plural form—"you" and its conjugations—was used as a sign of deference to authority. This is, for example, analogous but not identical to the difference between *tú* and *usted* in Spanish. While we removed these pronouns, we want you to appreciate that the early to middle modern English authors were trying to convey something contrary to what you might have initially believed. They were amplifying the personal nature of the Lord God—that God enters into a covenant relationship with his people and knows them by name. While that linguistic expression has been lost in our modern renderings, we hope you will read the older versions with fresh eyes, appreciating the intimacy these authors enjoyed with our Lord God.

Organization

To help the reader find certain prayers, we have adopted two organizational systems in this book. The first is a set of numbers that allow us to reference the prayer (1 to 100) and the historical introduction (✿ 1–40). Those numbers can be seen in each individual entry as well as in the author and topic indexes. Further, we have created our own titles for each prayer in order to help readers anticipate the content of the prayer. These are also listed in the front matter of this book. However, when discussing a particular prayer in the historical introductions, we have adopted the tried-and-true practice of using the first line of the modern English version (in quotation marks) as a way to refer to the entire prayer.

Suggestions for Use
For Personal Devotion

When this work was conceived, one of our main concerns was to make it as accessible as possible. Yet, the content of these prayers needed no help in this area, as all believers experience deep sorrows and joys throughout their lives and bring these all to God in prayer. All of the prayers in this collection were authored by real people who went through many ups and downs, and we were careful to select prayers that represent this variety. Our hope is that as you read these prayers, you will be comforted and encouraged by how God has preserved their authors, who walked through both valleys and mountains, to the very end.

For example, Samuel Johnson wrote his grieving prayer that begins "Almighty and most merciful Father" after the death of his wife in order to prepare himself to celebrate Easter. John of Damascus's "With pain earth's joys are mingled" confesses that the pains of this world are real but fade in light of God's eternal blessing. Other prayers are deeply theological, written to stir the heart to catch up to what the mind already knows from Scripture. Bede's "Be near to me, my only hope" is densely doctrinal, yet in it he models how doctrine moves through prayer toward worship. Our chief hope is that as you read these prayers, you will meditate on how the authors faced life under the bright light of the gospel.

In total, there are one hundred prayers in this work. This means you could, for example, read one prayer per day for three months and meditate on how the original author reflected on a certain circumstance in light of Christ's death and resurrection. Alternatively, you could also use the topic index to find a relevant subject, turn to the listed prayers, and meditate on how different authors approached the same subject.

As a Template for Prayer

As this project progressed, another hope developed: we hoped these prayers would serve as templates for readers to use in order to bring greater depth, piety, and devotion to their personal prayer lives. When Zach was in Bible college, he had a professor who encouraged candidates for ministry to work hard to teach people how they should pray. He would say things like, "If our people don't know better, all they will do is pray for their cat and their physical ailment."[7] Now, that same professor would never deny that God cares about those things; indeed, not even a hair can fall from our head apart from God's providential care. However, this professor had a point. In our experience, we have had so few models of doctrinally informed prayer that we struggle to know how to pray for things beyond what is in front of us. We often need someone to show us how to pray more deeply, boldly, and with ever-increasing confidence.

Consider for a moment how the disciples regularly heard the morning prayers of their mothers and fathers, rabbinical prayers in the synagogues, and Jesus's prayers in his early ministry. Yet, when they had a moment alone with him, they still asked him to teach them how to pray. We always need discipleship in our prayer life.

Further, using these prayers as templates can add variety to your devotional time. In fact, some of these prayers were originally designed to be templates. For example, Isaac Watts said that the purpose of his prayer book was to provide a framework for prayer in order to guide readers in their own prayers. In "Oh Lord God most high and most holy," Watts even included section headings so that individuals would

---

7 This quotation is from the editor's personal experience.

know the various components that a prayer can include. Thus, you could, for instance, follow Watts's template, replacing generalities with loved ones' names and other specific details. You could also take a prayer such as Anselm's "Come, oh come, most gracious comforter of afflicted souls," read one or two lines, and then express how that line is either already true in your life or represents a sincere longing for it to become true.

In a Public Setting

There are also prayers in this work that were meant to be read before a congregation as part of public worship of the gathered church. We hope those prayers will benefit pastors and ministers leading public worship. Interested leaders should be assured that each of these prayers confesses an orthodox faith.

Further, like William Jay's hopes for his own prayer book, we also hope our prayer book will aid parents and guardians in the spiritual instruction of their children and family worship within their homes. Adults who may be intimidated by leading children in prayer can begin by simply reading a prayer with a heart aimed toward pleasing God and not impressing anyone else. Those of us who grew up without such spiritual instruction have to start somewhere. If a child asks questions about the content of any of these prayers, you can probably find the answer in the historical catechisms. We recommend Chad Van Dixhoorn's *Creeds, Confessions, and Catechisms*,[8] which introduces the Heidelberg and Westminster Catechisms. These are trustworthy expositions of the Christian faith. Being Baptists, the editors are also partial to the readily available "Baptist Catechism" commonly attributed to Benjamin Keach.[9] As children continue to mature, parents can then lean into using our collection of prayers as a template for family worship.

However you choose to use this work, we hope it will equip you as one of

the saints for the work of ministry, for building up the body of Christ, until we all attain to the unity of the faith and of the knowledge of the Son of God, to mature manhood, to the measure of the stature of the fullness of Christ, so that we may no longer be children, tossed to and fro by the waves and carried about by every wind of doctrine, by human cunning, by craftiness in deceitful schemes. (Eph. 4:12–14)

8   Chad Van Dixhoorn, *Creeds, Confessions, and Catechisms: A Reader's Edition* (Wheaton, IL: Crossway, 2022).

9   William Collins and Benjamin Keach, *The Baptist Catechism: Or, a Brief Instruction in the Principles of the Christian Religion* (London: Printed for and sold by Joseph Marshall at the Bible in Newgate-Street, 1720).

PART 1

PRAYERS

1

Early Church (100–800)

1. The Model Prayer

Jesus of Nazareth, Luke 11:2–4

He said to them, "When you pray, say:

'Father, hallowed be your name.
Your kingdom come.
Give us each day our daily bread,
and forgive us our sins,
    for we ourselves forgive everyone who is indebted
        to us.
And lead us not into temptation.'"

2. Prayer for Loved Ones
Paul the apostle, Philippians 1:3–11

I thank my God in all my remembrance of you, always in every prayer of mine for you all making my prayer with joy, because of your partnership in the gospel from the first day until now. And I am sure of this, that he who began a good work in you will bring it to completion at the day of Jesus Christ. It is right for me to feel this way about you all, because I hold you in my heart, for you are all partakers with me of grace, both in my imprisonment and in the defense and confirmation of the gospel. For God is my witness, how I yearn for you all with the affection of Christ Jesus. And it is my prayer that your love may abound more and more, with knowledge and all discernment, so that you may approve what is excellent, and so be pure and blameless for the day of Christ, filled with the fruit of righteousness that comes through Jesus Christ, to the glory and praise of God.

3. Prayer of Thanksgiving
The Didache (ca. 100) ❧ *1*

Holy Father, we thank you for your holy name, which you have caused to dwell in our hearts. And we thank you for the knowledge and faith and immortality that you have made

4

known to us through Jesus, your servant. To you be glory forever.

You, the Almighty Lord of all, created everything for the sake of your name. You have given food and drink to humanity for their enjoyment so that they would give you thanks. But to us, you have given spiritual food and drink and eternal life through your servant. Above all, we give thanks to you because you are all powerful. To you be glory forever.

Remember, oh Lord, your church, to deliver her from all evil and to perfect her in your love. Gather her from the four winds once she has been sanctified for the kingdom you have prepared for her, for yours is the power and glory forever.

May grace arrive and let this world pass away. Hosanna to the God of David. If anyone is holy, let him come. If he is not, let him repent. *Maranatha.* Amen.

4. Prayer of Hope for the Congregation
Clement of Rome (d. ca. 99) ❧ *2*

Grant us, Lord God, a hope in the fount of all creation, your name. Open the eyes of our hearts that we may know you, the highest of the highest, the Holy One who rests among the holy. You are the one who humbles the hubris of the proud, who destroys the philosophies of the nations, who exalts the truly humble to the highest position and lowers the self-exalted, the one who brings wealth and causes poverty, the one who takes life away and makes life happen, the only protector of souls, and the God of all flesh. You are the one who gazes into the unknown depths, who attends the works of humanity, who helps those in danger, the Savior of the hopeless, the creator and overseer of all spirits. You are the one who increases the nations of the earth, and from them all, you have called those who love you through Jesus Christ, your beloved Son, by whom you have discipled, purified, and esteemed us.

We beg of you, Lord, be our helper and our protector. Save those of us who are afflicted, show mercy to the humble, lift up those who have fallen, reveal yourself to the needy, heal the sick, and bring back those of your people who have strayed from your path. Nourish the hungry, redeem our captives, build up the weak, and comfort the discouraged. Let all the peoples know you, that you alone are God, that Jesus Christ is your Son, and we are your people, the sheep of your pasture, for you have revealed the timeless foundation of the cosmos through your works. You, Lord, created the world. You are faithful to all generations, righteous in your judgments, wondrous in your power and majesty. You are skillful in what you create and wise in establishing what will be. You are shown to be good in what is seen and kind to those who find their confidence in you. In your mercy and compassion, forgive us for our lawlessness, our unrighteousness, our wrongdoings, our faults.

Consider none of the sins of your male slaves and female slaves. Cleanse us with the washing of your truth and direct our steps that we may proceed with devout hearts so that we may do what is good and pleasing to you and to our rulers.

Yes, Lord, reveal your face to us in peace for our benefit so that we may be covered by your mighty hand and rescued from all our sins by your sovereign arm. Rescue us from those who hate us unjustly. Grant harmony and peace to us and to all the residents of this earth, just as you granted to our fathers when they devoutly called on you in faith and truth. And grant that we may be obedient to your almighty and most honored name and to our earthly rulers and congregational leaders.

You, Lord, have given our leaders the authority to rule by your magnificent and indescribable power so that we may comprehend the glory and honor you have given them, but also so that we may be subject to them, not fighting against your will. Lord, give them health, peace, harmony, and stability so that they might righteously oversee the stewardship you have given them.

For you, Lord, heavenly, eternal King, grant to us (mere humans) glory, honor, and authority over the earthly creatures.

You, Lord God, direct our plans according to what is good and pleasing to you so that when we righteously govern, in peace and gentleness, the stewardship you have given us, we may experience your mercy. You who alone has the ability to accomplish all of these things for us and to do what is even more exceedingly good, we praise you through the high priest and defender (protector, patron) of our souls, Jesus Christ, through whom the glory and majesty be yours now and for all generations and for all time. Amen.

5. Prayer of Intercession
Polycarp (69–155) ❧ *3*

May God, the Father of our Lord Jesus Christ, the eternal high priest, build you up in faith and truth and in all meekness, without anger, with patience and long-suffering and tolerance and self-control. May he grant you an inheritance among his saints. And may he grant that to us also and to all who will believe in our Lord and God Jesus Christ and in his Father who raised him from the dead.

6. Prayer of Martyrdom
Polycarp (69–155) ❧ *3*

Oh Lord God Almighty, Father of your beloved and blessed Son, Jesus Christ, by whom we have received the knowledge of you, the God of angels and powers and of every creature, and of the whole race of the righteous who live before you: I give thanks that you have counted me worthy of this day and this hour, that I should have a part in the number of your martyrs, a part in Christ's cup, that I may be brought into the resurrection to eternal life, both of soul and body, through the incorruption imparted by the Holy Spirit.

I pray that my death may be received as an acceptable sacrifice, just as you, the ever-truthful God, have foreordained, having revealed it beforehand to me. Now you have fulfilled it. Thus, I praise you for all things, I bless you, and I glorify you along with the everlasting and heavenly Jesus Christ, your beloved Son, with whom to you and the Holy Spirit be glory both now and for all coming ages. Amen.

7. Prayer for the Church
Hippolytus of Rome (ca. 170–ca. 235) 🔖 *4*

We ask that you send the Holy Spirit as a holy offering to the holy church. As we assemble, give to all the saints the fullness of the Holy Spirit for the confirmation of true faith so that we may praise and glorify you through your Son, Jesus Christ, through whom glory and honor to the Father and the Son with the Holy Spirit in your holy church are yours now and forever! Amen.

8. Prayer before Receiving the Lord's Supper
The Clementine Liturgy ❧ 5

Oh great and mighty God, unequaled in counsel and in all your mighty works, the God and Father of your holy Son, Jesus, our Savior: Look upon us, your flock, whom you have chosen through him to the glory of your name. Sanctify us in body and soul. Grant that we would be purified from all depravity of the flesh and spirit and that we may receive your good gifts, not having been judged to be unworthy. Be our helper, supporter, and protector through your Christ, with whom to you and to the Holy Spirit be glory, honor, praise, and thanksgiving forever. Amen.

9. Prayer for Enemies
The Clementine Liturgy ❧ 5

We pray for those who hate us and persecute us for the sake of your name, for those who are outside of the church and those who have gone astray. Please convert them to the good and turn away their anger.

10. Prayer for Divine Strength
The Clementine Liturgy ❧ 5

Oh Lord God Almighty, who hears the prayers of the upright, we give thanks to you, that you have chosen in your unbreakable will to make us partakers of your holy mysteries, which you have given to us for the full assurance of those things that we rightly know for our preservation in godliness and for the remission of our sins—for the name of Christ has been placed upon us, and we are united to you.

You have called us to be separated from the corrupting influence of the ungodly. Please unite us with those who have been set apart for you. Establish us firmly in the truth by the presence and work of the Holy Spirit. Where ignorance remains in us, please reveal your truth. Supply us in our lacking. Strengthen us in the truth we have already grasped. Preserve the ministers of your gospel, keeping them blameless in your service.

For our earthly authorities, we ask that you keep them in peace and righteousness. Grant us all a favorable climate so that the fruits of the ground would be plentiful. By your all-powerful providence, preserve the entire world, which you hold and maintain in the palm of your hand. Pacify the nations that seem to delight in war.

For your church, we ask that you convert those who remain in error. Sanctify your people. Preserve those who are single, still in virginity. Those who are married, keep them faithful to their spouses and to their marriage vows.

For those who have been given the honor of remaining unmarried, dedicated to you, strengthen them in their chastity.

Protect our children so they may grow into adulthood. Confirm those who have newly believed your gospel. Instruct those who are young in the faith and make them worthy of full communion with your people. Gather us all into your heavenly kingdom in Christ Jesus our Lord. To you, with him and the Holy Spirit, be glory, honor, and adoration, now and forever. Amen.

11. Prayer for Peace

The Syrian Clementine Liturgy ❧ *6*

Oh God, the unfathomable abyss of peace, the inexpressible sea of love, the fount of all blessings, and the affectionate Father, the one who sends peace to all who receive it, we ask that you would open to us the depths of your love and saturate us with the overflowing streams of riches from your grace. Make us children of calm and heirs of peace. Ignite in us the fire of your love. Enkindle in us a true reverence for you. In your power, strengthen us in our weakness. Keep us close to you and join us to each other with a firm bond of unity. We ask all of this for the sake of Jesus Christ. Amen.

12. Prayer for Gifts from God

The Liturgy of Saint Chrysostom ❧ 7

Almighty God, who has given us the grace necessary for us to make our common requests with one accord and who promises that when two or three are gathered together in your name you will grant their requests, we ask that you would fulfill the godly desires and petitions of your servants, as you deem best for them, granting in this world knowledge of your truth and, in the world to come, life everlasting. Amen.

13. Prayer for the People of God

The Liturgy of Saint Chrysostom ❧ 7

Dear Lord, remember this city where your people dwell and every other city and country with your faithful followers in them. Oh Lord, remember all who sail and those who travel by land, those who are sick or who are close to death, and those who are captives in need of freedom. Remember, oh Lord, those who display good fruit, those who cultivate the soil of your holy church and do not neglect the poor. Grant that, in unity of voice and heart, we may glorify and praise your great and majestic name—Father, Son, and Holy Spirit—both now and forevermore. Amen.

14. Prayer for Holiness for Old and New Believers
Old Gallican Rite ❧ *8*

Grant holiness to new believers, oh Father. Give knowledge to the ignorant. Give aid to those who are running their course. Give sorrow to those who have erred without knowledge. Give passion to those who are lukewarm. To those who are mature, give a good ending. We ask all of this for the sake of Christ Jesus, our Lord. Amen.

15. Prayer before Publicly Reading Scripture
Old Gallican Rite ❧ *8*

May Jesus, our God, the first and the last, living unto the ages of ages, the one who holds the keys of death and hell, grant you who are about to read a pure heart and pure lips and a voice like a loud trumpet to announce the word to impure spirits. For those who are about to hear, open our ears, oh Lord, that we may understand what the Spirit says to the church. Amen.

16. Prayer for Peace
Old Gallican Rite ❧ *8*

Lord Jesus Christ, you said to your apostles, "I leave you with peace. My peace I give to you" [John 14:27], so we ask that you would look not on our weakness but rather look on the faith of your church. Draw her closer in peace and unity according to your will, oh lover of humanity, who lives and reigns with the Father and the Holy Spirit unto the end of the ages. Amen.

17. Prayer for Protection
Old Gallican Rite ✺ *8*

Being delivered from evil, being strengthened always in the good, we ought always to serve you, our God and our Lord. Put an end, oh Lord, to our sins at their very core. Give joy to the afflicted, liberty to the captives, health to the sick, rest to the dead. Grant peace and security in all our days.

Break the boldness of our enemies. Hear, oh God, the prayers of all your faithful Christian servants in this day and time. We ask this through our Lord Jesus Christ, your Son, who lives and reigns with you in the unity of the Holy Spirit, God throughout all ages. Amen.

18. Prayer of Praise
Old Gallican Rite ✺ *8*

It is right and just, indeed it is fair and just, for us to praise you, to bless you, to thank you, almighty and everlasting God, the one who takes glory in the assembly of the saints, those whom you have sealed with the spiritual blessing before the foundations of the world. They are the same ones whom you adopted as heirs with the only begotten by his incarnation and by the redemptive work of the cross. They are the ones in whom your Holy Spirit reigns, some of whom have come to the glory of a blessed martyrdom by your holy favor.

19. Prayer of Thanksgiving for the Forgiveness of Sins
Old Gallican Rite ❧ 8

It is right and just for us to give thanks to you, holy Lord, almighty Father, eternal God, through Jesus Christ your Son, our Lord, whom you offered as a sacrifice for us all. Oh, the wonderful condescension of your mercy to us! Oh, the inexpressible love! In order to redeem the slave, you gave your Son! Oh, surely the sin of Adam—which was destroyed by the death of Christ—was a necessary and even, dare we say, happy fault, for because of its magnitude, it deserved to have a redeemer! Without it, we would never know the greatness of your love, for by it, you proved your love by the death of your only begotten, coeternal Son, our Lord and our God, Jesus Christ. The condescension of your holiness overcame the evil of the devil—for where sin abounded, your grace abounded even more. But you, in your mercy, have restored to us more than the jealous enemy had taken. He longs for paradise; you offer the heavens. He brought temporal death; you have given eternal life. Therefore, the entire world praises you with exuberant joy, joining with the angelic choir that unceasingly sings hymns of your glory.

20. Prayer for Church Growth
Old Gallican Rite ❧ 8

It is truly right and just to pray with enthusiasm and with one accord to the almighty God and in unity with his only Son, the Lord Jesus Christ, our Savior, who delivered his church from the second death by his blood that was shed on the cross. Through him, we beg of you, Almighty God, that you would grow your church in faith, guard her in hope, protect her in love, and be willing to accept her sacrifices with glory and honor.

21. Prayer for Family and Friends
Old Gallican Rite ❧ 8

Have mercy, oh Lord, on all those whom you have associated with us in the bonds of friendship and family. Grant that they, with us, may be so perfectly conformed to your holy will that, being cleansed from all sin, we may be found worthy, by the inspiration of your love, to participate together in the blessedness of your heavenly kingdom through Jesus Christ our Lord. Amen.

22. Prayer at Mealtimes
Old Gallican Rite ❧ 8

Abba, Father, fulfill the office of your name toward your servants. Govern, protect, preserve, sanctify, guide, and console us. Let us be so enkindled with love for you that we may not be despised by you, oh most merciful Lord, most tender Father. We pray these things for Jesus Christ's sake. Amen.

23. Prayer for a Pure Heart
Liturgy of Jerusalem and Saint James ❧ 9

Help us, oh Lord, lover of humanity. Freely and without condemnation, grant us a pure heart to call on you, the Holy God who is in the heavens, and together pray as our Lord instructed us.

24. Prayer for Sanctification
Liturgy of Jerusalem and Saint James ❧ 9

Oh Lord, Jesus Christ, the Son of the living God, the lamb and the shepherd who takes away the sin of the world, who graciously canceled what the two debtors owed, who pardoned the woman who was a sinner, who not only forgave the sins of the paralyzed man but also cured him of his disease, oh God, remit, pardon, and forgive the sins we have committed both willfully and against our will, knowingly or through ignorance, by active and passive disobedience. Certainly, the Holy Spirit knows the extent of our guilt. Whether these sins came about merely because of our human nature as sojourners in this fallen world or because we have been led astray by the deceit of the devil or because we have been the recipients of a curse or imprecation, we pray and beg of you that because of your ineffable love for humanity, we may be absolved by your decree and released from any oath or imprecation against us.

Oh God, please act according to your great goodness. Even so, oh Lord, hear my supplication for your servants. Because you do not delight in remembering evil, overlook all their offenses. Forgive all their sins—both voluntary and involuntary—and deliver them from eternal punishment, for you are the one who told us that whatever we loose on earth will be loosed in heaven. You are our God, a God who has the power to have mercy, to save, and to forgive sins. To you, Jesus, along with the unbegotten Father and the life-giving Spirit, belong glory, now and forevermore, world without end. Amen.

25. Prayer for Sanctification
Liturgy of Jerusalem and Saint James ❧ *9*

Oh good God, by the grace of Christ and the descent of your most Holy Spirit, sanctify our souls, bodies, and spirits. Search our minds and examine our consciences. Put away from us all evil notions, all impure thoughts, all filthy lusts, all indecent thoughts, all envy, all pride, all hypocrisy, all falsehood and deceit, all worldly cares, all covetousness, all excessive vanity, all laziness, all malice, all wrath, all anger, all memories of injuries committed against us, all evil speaking, and every movement of flesh and spirit that is contrary to your holy will.

26. Prayer for Blessing
Liturgy of Saint Mark ❧ *10*

We beg of you, oh lover of humanity, to bless all of your people, the flocks of your fold. Send into their hearts the peace that only comes from heaven, and grant all of us also the peace of this life. Give authentic, deep life to all of our souls, and let no deadly sin prevail against us or any of your people. Deliver all who are facing troubles, for you are our God, the only one who can set the captives free, who gives hope to the hopeless and help to the helpless, the one who lifts up the fallen and is the haven of the shipwrecked.

Grant your pity, your pardon, and your refreshment to every Christian soul, whether in affliction or in error. Preserve us from hurt and danger during our journey through this life and grant that we may end our lives as believing Christians who are well-pleasing to you. Keep us free from sin so that we may have our inheritance with all your saints. Amen.

27. Prayer for Illumination
Liturgy of Saint Mark ❧ *10*

Oh God of light, Father of life, author of grace, creator of worlds, source of all knowledge, giver of wisdom, protector of our souls: To the faint of heart who trust in you, you give those things the angels desire to know. Oh sovereign Lord, who has brought us up from the depths of darkness into the light, who has given us life from death, who has graciously granted us freedom from slavery, and who, through the presence of the only begotten Son, has scattered the darkness of sin that lies within us, please, we ask of you, send your all-holy Spirit to open our eyes that we may understand and to sanctify us wholly in soul, body, and spirit. Amen.

28. Prayer to Begin the Day
Liturgy of Saint Mark ❧ *10*

We give you thanks—more than thanks, oh Lord our God— for all your goodness in all times and in all places. You have shielded, rescued, helped, and guided us all the days of our lives. And you have brought us to this very hour.

We pray and beg of you, merciful God, to grant in your goodness that we may spend this day, and all the days of our lives, without sin, in fullness of joy, holiness, and reverence for you. Please drive away from us, oh Lord, all envy, fear, and temptations.

Give us what is good and right. In your mercy, please pardon whatever sins we commit in thought, word, or deed. Lead us not into temptation, but deliver us from evil; through the grace, mercy, and love of your only begotten Son. Amen.

29. Prayer for Love
The Coptic Liturgy of Saint Cyril ⮞ *11*

Oh God of love who has given a new commandment through your only begotten Son—that we should love one another even as you loved us, though we were unworthy wanderers—and gave your beloved Son for our life and salvation, we pray, Lord, in every season of our life on earth, give to us, your servants, a mind forgetful of past ill will, a pure conscience with sincere desires, and a heart to love our brothers and sisters. Do this, we ask, for the sake of Jesus Christ, your Son, our Lord and only Savior. Amen.

30. A Doxology
Cyprian (ca. 210–258) ⮞ *12*

Christ imparts this saving gracious pardon. This gift of mercy he grants to us by overcoming death in his victory on the cross, redeeming the believer at the price of his own blood, reconciling humanity to his God and Father, and restoring mortal humanity to life through heavenly regeneration. May we all follow him. Let us be enrolled as citizens by taking his oath and living under his standard.

This is he who opened to us the way of life. This is he who makes possible our return to paradise. This is he who leads us to the kingdom of heaven. With him we will live forever, having been made through him children of God. With him we will rejoice forever, having been restored through his own blood. As Christians, we will be at once glorified alongside Christ, blessed by God the Father, rejoicing always in God's sight with an unfailing pleasure, and rightly giving all to God, for no rightful subject of death who through the promise of immortality has been set free from the fear of death can be anything other than joyful and grateful.

31. A Doxology
Cyprian (ca. 210–258) ❧ *12*

Let us rouse ourselves as much as we are able, beloved brothers and sisters. Ending the drowsiness of past slumber, let us stay alert so that we may observe and keep the teachings of the Lord. We should strive to be the people he taught us to be when he said, "Be dressed for action and keep your lamps burning brightly. Behave like men waiting for their Lord so that when he does come and knocks at the door, it may be opened for him. Blessed are those servants the Lord finds ready and waiting with expectation" [Luke 12:35–38]. We must remain prepared or else, when the day of departure comes, we will find ourselves overly burdened and entangled by the things of this world.

May we let the light of our good works shine so brightly around us that it may lead us from the night of this world to the light of eternal brightness. Let us await the sudden return of the Lord in such a way that when he knocks, our faith may be seen to be vigilant, ready to receive from the Lord the reward due for our watchfulness.

If these commands are kept, if these warnings are heeded, if these teachings are maintained, the deceitful enemy will not be able to overwhelm us while we are sleeping. We will surely reign as vigilant servants with Christ as our Lord.

32. Prayer before Preaching and Teaching the Holy Scriptures
Hilary of Poitiers (ca. 310–ca. 367) ❧ *13*

I know, oh Lord God Almighty, that as the chief duty of my life, I owe you the devotion of all my words and thoughts. The gift of speech that you have given can bring no higher reward than the opportunity of service in preaching you and displaying you as you truly are—as Father and Father of God the only begotten. I long to display you to the world even in its blindness and to the heretic in his rebellion. But this is the mere expression of my own desire, if I am being honest. I must pray also for the gift of your help and compassion, that the breath of your Spirit may fill the sails of faith and confession that I have spread and that you would send a favorable wind to aid me on my voyage of instruction. We can trust the promise of him who said, "Ask and it shall be given you; seek and you shall find; knock and it shall be opened for you" [Matt. 7:7]. Thus, in our need, we will pray for your help. We will bring an untiring energy to the study of your prophets and apostles, and we will knock for entrance at every gate of hidden knowledge. But it is yours to answer these prayers, to grant the things we seek, to open the doors upon which we knock.

Our minds at birth are dulled with clouded vision; our feeble intellect is penned with the barriers of an impassable ignorance about divine things. But the study of your revelation elevates our souls to the understanding of sacred truth, and obedience to the faith is the path to a certainty beyond the reach of unassisted reason.

Therefore, we look to your support for the first trembling steps of this undertaking. We look to your aid that our very walk may gain strength and prosper. We look to you to give us the fellowship of the same Spirit who guided the prophets and the apostles that we may take their words in the sense in which they spoke them and assign the right meaning to every utterance, for we will speak of things that they preached in mystery. We will speak of you, oh God eternal, Father of the eternal and only begotten God. We will speak of you alone who are without beginning and of the one Lord Jesus Christ, begotten of you from everlasting. We may not sever him from you or make him one of a plurality of gods on any plea of difference of your natures. We may not say that he is not begotten of you because you are one. We must not fail to confess him as true God, seeing that he is begotten of you, true God, his Father.

Grant us, therefore, precision of language, soundness of argument, grace of style, and loyalty to truth. Enable us to utter the things that we believe so that—as the prophets and apostles have taught us—we may confess you, one God, our Father, and one Lord Jesus Christ. Thereby we will put to silence the gainsaying of heretics.

33. Doxology on the Incarnation

Ephrem the Syrian (ca. 306–373) ❧ *14*

Glory to you who clothed yourself in Adam's mortal body and made it a fountain of life for all mortals. You are he who lives, for those who killed you were but gardeners to your life—they planted it as a seed in the depths of the earth that it may rise and raise up many with it.

Come, let us make our love the great censer of the community and offer our hymns and prayers as incense to the one who made his own cross a censer for the Godhead, offering it on behalf of all of us.

He that was from above condescended to those who were below to give his own treasures to them. Thus, though the needy drew near to his humanity, they received the gift from his divinity. Therefore, he made the body that he put on the treasurer of his riches so that he might bring them out of the Lord's storehouse and distribute them to the needy, his very brothers and sisters.

Glory be to him who received from us in order that he might give to us so that through what is ours we might more abundantly receive of what is rightly his! Indeed, through that mediator, humanity was able to receive life from its Savior, as through an earlier mediator it had received death from its killer. You, oh Lord, are the one who made for yourself the body of a servant so that through it you might give to those who long for you all that they desire. Moreover, in you were made visible the hidden wishes of them who killed and buried you through the very fact that you clothed yourself in a body, for taking the opportunity afforded by your body, your killers murdered you, and those sinners were put to death by you so that, in taking the opportunity afforded by your body, those who buried you could be raised up with you. The power that may not be handled came down and clothed itself in a body that can be touched in order that the needy may draw near to him and that, in touching his humanity, they may understand his divinity.

34. Prayer for Godly Singing and Speaking
Ephrem the Syrian (ca. 306–373) ✿ *14*

Whatever is allowed, let us sing, Lord, with instruments and in the open. Let us not utter anything that is not permitted, seeing these are but the instruments of frail creatures. Lord, let my tongue be a pen for your glory, and let the finger of your grace use it to write words that are edifying. The pen, Lord, cannot write of its own accord. It needs someone to write with it. In the same way, please do not let my tongue begin to speak without you. Let it be an instrument in your hand. Specifically, do not let it be used to say anything that is not edifying. Indeed, praises be to your teaching!

35. Prayer for Heretics
Gregory of Nazianzus (329–390) ✿ *15*

May the only one who has the power to unite those who are at odds and free those who are bound, and who can empower our minds to escape the stranglehold of the ungodly dogma of heretical teachings, change these teachers into faithful followers rather than mere debaters, true Christians rather than in name only.

This is precisely what we beg of Christ because of his work: be reconciled to God; do not quench the Spirit. Even better, may Christ be reconciled to you, and may the Holy Spirit pull back the veil from your mind's eye.

But if you are too drawn to your pointless arguments, we at any rate will hold fast to the Trinity, and by the triune God we will be saved, remaining pure and blameless until the more perfect revealing of what we truly desire, Christ himself our Lord, to whom be the glory for ever and ever. Amen.

36. A Morning Prayer
Gregory of Nazianzus (329–390) ❧ *15*

As the sun rises, I lift my hand to you, oh God, for you to determine my path. Please control my passions. Help me stand firm in your ways and live this day for you. Allow no dark words, no sin-filled acts, no base thoughts even to enter my life. Rather, watch over all my internal actions so that I may truly keep my vow to you.

Please keep me from bringing shame to myself or, more importantly, to your people. Indeed, let your will be done through the grace that you give to me. Amen.

37. Prayer of Dedication for Children

Gregory of Nyssa (ca. 335–ca. 395), quoting
Emmelia of Caesarea (d. 375) ❧ *16*

To you, oh Lord, I offer my first and last children. This is my firstborn, and this is my last child. To you, both have been consecrated by law, and they are offerings to you. So sanctify them for your service. Amen.

38. Deathbed Prayer

Gregory of Nyssa (ca. 335–ca. 395), quoting
Macrina the Younger (d. 379) ❧ *16*

Oh Lord, you have removed the fear of death from me. You have changed the end of this earthly life into the beginning of true life for us. You allow our bodies to slumber for a while, only to be awakened at the sound of the last trumpet. You entrust our bodies of mere dust to the ground, all of which you formed with your own hands. And you restore even greater what you have already given, graciously transforming what is mortal and deformed in us.

You have delivered us from the curse and from sin, having become both for us. You have crushed the head of the serpent, who because of the chasm of our disobedience had grasped humanity by the throat. You have brought forth the resurrection. You have broken the gates of hell, and you have vanquished the one who held the power of death. You have given those who rightly fear you the reminder of the holy cross for the removal of the enemy and for the safety of daily life.

Oh eternal God, my God even from my mother's womb, whom my soul has loved with all its strength, to whom I have dedicated my body and soul from my youth even unto this very day, please send an angel of light to lead me to the place of repose where I can find the refreshing waters near the saints who have come before me.

You have cut through the flaming sword and brought to paradise the man who was crucified with you, the one who begged for your mercy. Please remember me also in your kingdom for I have been crucified with you and have disciplined my flesh out of a righteous fear of you and out of concern for your judgments.

Do not let the dreadful chasm separate me from your chosen ones. Do not let the adversary steal my offering. Do not let my sin be revealed before your eyes if I have been overwhelmed by my own sinfulness in any way, whether by word, by deed, or by corrupt understanding. Amen.

39. Prayer for Knowledge of God

Augustine of Hippo (354–430) ❧ *17*

You, oh Lord, are great and worthy of exceeding praise. Your great virtue and your wisdom are beyond comprehension. Humanity, though merely creatures, longs to praise you—the same humanity that bears the weight of mortality, the testimony of sin, and the reminder that you resist the proud. Still, humanity, this small part of your creation, inherently desires to praise you. You enkindle in us a longing to praise you because you have made us for yourself, and our hearts are restless until they rest in you.

Lord, let me know, let me truly comprehend, whether I should first come to you in prayer or with praise, whether I am to know you first or I should pray before I know you. But who calls to you without first knowing you? For the one who tries may unknowingly turn to another, mistaking that other for you. Or should you be called upon first in order that you may be known? But how will anyone call upon you if they do not first believe? How will they believe without a proclaimer? But those who seek him will praise the Lord, for those who seek him will find him. Those who find him will indeed praise him.

Let me seek you, then, Lord, even as I pray to you. Let me call upon you even as I believe in you, for you have been proclaimed to me. Oh Lord, my faith calls out to you—my faith that you have given, that you have inspired in me through the incarnation of your Son and through the ministry of your preacher.

40. Prayer regarding God's Apparent Silence
Augustine of Hippo (354–430) ❧ *17*

My God, how could I think that you were silent when I was the one who left you? Were you ever actually silent? Whose words were those if not yours that came to my ears through my mother, your faithful servant? Her words seemed like nothing more than a mother's unsolicited advice, which I would have been ashamed to heed. Little did I know those words were actually from you. I thought you were being silent when in reality you spoke through her words. In ignoring her, I was despising you.

41. Prayer for Mercy
Augustine of Hippo (354–430) ❧ *17*

Oh Lord, have mercy on me! I do not hide my wounds. You are a doctor; I am sick. You are merciful; I need mercy. Is not human life on earth merely a trial? Who actually wants troubles and problems? You command us to tolerate them, not to love them. No one loves what they merely endure, even if they love the endurance itself. Although they are glad to endure, they prefer not to suffer.

When I am in the midst of adversity, I long for success. When I am successful, I fear the coming adversity. Where is the middle ground where human life is not a constant trial? Woe to the prosperity of the world with its fear of adversity and corruption of joy! Woe to the adversities of the world—once, twice, and even a third time—with their desire for prosperity, because adversity itself is hard and also because it threatens to destroy endurance! Isn't human life on earth merely a constant trial?

42. Prayer after a Sermon
Augustine of Hippo (354–430) ❧ *17*

We turn our hearts to the Lord God, the Father Almighty, and we offer to him with pure hearts—so far as our depravity will allow—true thanks. With all our hearts we beg of his exceeding kindness that out of his good pleasure, he would be willing to hear our prayers. We ask that by his power, he would drive out the enemy from our deeds and thoughts, that he would increase our faith, guide our understanding, give us thoughts centered on him, and lead us to his true joy through Jesus Christ, his Son, our Lord, who lives and reigns with him in the unity of the Holy Spirit: one God, forever and ever. Amen.

43. Prayer for Divine Approval

Augustine of Hippo (354–430) ❧ *17*

When we reach you, these many things we have said that fall short of you will cease. And yet you will remain "all in all" [1 Cor. 15:28]. And we will say one thing that will not end, praising you as unified. In you, we also will become one. Oh Lord, one God, triune God, may you acknowledge as your own whatever I have said of you. Whatever I have said of my own accord, may it be forgiven both by you and by your people. Amen.

44. Prayer for Responding to Heretics

John Cassian (ca. 360–ca. 435) ❧ *18*

Laying our hands upon that monstrous head of the deadly serpent, and longing to lay hold of all the limbs that are entangled in the huge folds and coils of his body, again and again, we pray to you. Oh Lord Jesus, to whom we have always prayed, we ask that you would give us words by opening our mouths so that we may pull down the strongholds, destroy evil counsels and every height that exalts itself against the true knowledge of God, and bring into captivity every thought so that every single one might be obedient to you, for indeed, only the one who has been taken captive by you may be said to be truly free.

We ask that you would be present in your divine work and with those of yours who are striving for you beyond the feeble measure of their own strength. Let us bruise the gaping mouth of this new serpent as well as the neck that swells with deadly poison, oh you who make the feet of believers to tread unharmed on serpents and scorpions, walk among the adder and basilisk, and tread underfoot the lion and the dragon. Grant that, through the fearless boldness of steadfast innocence, the young child may play at the mouth of the asp's den and the weaned child may thrust his hand into the den of the basilisk.

Grant also to us that we may thrust our own hands unharmed into the den of this monstrous and most wicked basilisk. And if it has left behind a hiding place or a nest of eggs or even the remnants of its own slimy journey in any hole (such as in the human heart), please remove all the foul and deadly pollution of this noxious serpent.

Take away the uncleanness their blasphemy has brought on them, and purify with the fan of your holy cleansing the souls that have been plunged in rotting mud so that the dens of thieves may become houses of prayer. We pray that in the places where hedgehogs and monsters and satyrs and all kinds of strange creatures currently dwell, that there the gifts of your Holy Spirit—the beauty of faith and holiness—may shine brightly.

And as once you destroyed idolatry and cast out images and made shrines of virtue out of the temples of devils and let beams of light into the dens of serpents and scorpions, do once again make homes of beauty and splendor out of those dens of error and shame. Please pour the light of your compassion and truth on the eyes of all those who have been blinded by heretical obstinacy so that they may ultimately hold on to the life-giving mystery of your incarnation and so come to know you to have been born as very man of that sacred womb of a pure virgin and yet to acknowledge that you were always very God.

2

Medieval Church (800–1500)

45. Prayer for Faith

Bede (673–735) 19

Oh Lord our God, we believe in you, the Father and the Son and the Holy Spirit, for you could not truly say, "Go, baptize the nations in the name of the Father and of the Son and of the Holy Spirit" [Matt. 28:19] unless you were indeed the Trinity. Nor would you command us to be baptized, oh Lord God, in the name of one who is not actually the Lord God. Nor would you say with a divine voice, "Hear oh Israel, the Lord your God is one Lord" [Deut. 6:4] unless you were truly a Trinity, truly one Lord God.

Unless you were God the Father himself and Jesus Christ your Son, your Word, and the Holy Spirit your gift, we would not read in the true letters, "God sent his Son" [John 3:17].

Nor would you, the only begotten Son, say of the Holy Spirit, "whom the Father sends in my name and whom I will send to you from the Father" [John 14:26]. Thus, you have directed our attention to this rule of faith, the origin of all things, the most perfect beauty, and the most blessed delight.

46. Prayer for Protection
Bede (673–735) ❧ *19*

Savior of souls, Redeemer of the world, Jesus Christ, true God, immortal King: I, a mere sinner, beg your immense compassion that by your great mercy (which I sing about in the Psalms), you would free my soul from sin. Turn away my heart from all evil, all wicked and unfaithful thoughts. Free my body from its bondage to sin. Drive away from me carnal lust. Deliver me from every trap of Satan and of his ministers, both visible and invisible, the unfaithful enemies who seek my soul. Keep me from these and from all other evils, Savior of the world, who lives and reigns and rules with God the Father and the Holy Spirit, time without end. Amen.

47. Prayer in Praise of the Trinity
Bede (673–735) ❧ *19*

Be near to me, my only hope, oh Lord my God.
Be near in the true light, oh Father God Almighty.

Be near, Light of Light and Word and Son of God,
    God Almighty.
Be near in the harmony of the Holy Spirit, Father, and
    Son, God Almighty.
Be near, one God Almighty, Father and Son and Holy
    Spirit.
Teach us faith, stir up hope, instill love.
I will to be near, but this is not from me but
    from you.
To leave this world and the earth and to seek heaven
Is a weak thing to desire without your help.
Give me the wings of faith to fly up to you.
This faith in you, through you, about you, I confess.
That you are one in substance, a Trinity in persons,
    I confess.
That you are always the same, alive, and intelligent,
    I confess.
That you are three in one and one in three, I confess.
The Father and the Son and the Holy Spirit. Oh blessed
    Trinity.
God, Lord, Helper, oh blessed Trinity.
Love, Grace, Communion. Oh blessed Trinity.
Love of God, grace of Christ, communion of the Holy
    Spirit. Oh blessed Trinity.

Unbegotten one, begotten one, regenerating one.
> Oh blessed Trinity.

True Light, Light from Light, true enlightening one.
> Oh blessed Trinity.

Unseen invisibility, seen invisibility, unseen visibility.
> Oh blessed Trinity.

Fountain, river, source of water. Oh blessed Trinity.

From one all things, through one all things, in one all
> things. Oh blessed Trinity.

From whom, by whom, and in whom are all things.
> Oh blessed Trinity.

Living life, life from the living, giver of life. Oh blessed
> Trinity.

One from himself, one from one, one from both of
> them. Oh blessed Trinity.

One from himself, one from the other, one from both.
> Oh blessed Trinity.

But everything, everything always in three, and
> everything equally in each. Oh blessed Trinity.

The true Father, true Son, true Holy Spirit. Oh blessed
> Trinity.

One Father, the Logos, the Paraclete are one substance.
> Oh blessed Trinity.

All are one essence, one virtue, one goodness.
> Oh blessed Trinity.

God is blessed, in whom and by whom and through
> whom all things are blessed that are blessed.
> Oh blessed Trinity.

God is the true and greatest life, in whom and by whom
> and through whom all who truly live find their life.
> Oh blessed Trinity.

God is good and beautiful, in whom and by whom and
> through whom all good and beautiful things find
> their goodness and beauty. Oh blessed Trinity.

God, to whom faith awakens us, hope raises us up, love
> unites us. Oh blessed Trinity.

God who commands us to seek and to find and who
> opens to our knocking. Oh blessed Trinity.

God, above whom is nothing, outside of whom is
> nothing, without whom is nothing. Oh blessed
> Trinity.

God, under whom is everything, in whom is everything,
> with whom is everything. Oh blessed Trinity.

We call upon you, we adore you, we praise you.
> Oh blessed Trinity.

Hear us, hear us, hear us. Oh blessed Trinity.

Our hope, our salvation, our honor. Oh blessed Trinity.

Increase the faith in us, increase the hope, increase the
love. Oh blessed Trinity.

Free us, save us, justify us. Oh blessed Trinity.

Have mercy, Lord, for your mercy has freed us.
Oh blessed Trinity.

Have mercy, Lord, because we believe in you.
Oh blessed Trinity.

Have mercy, Lord, because by your mercy we believe
you. Oh blessed Trinity.

Have mercy, Lord, because by your mercy we hope in
you. Oh blessed Trinity.

Have mercy, Lord, because by your mercy we love you.
Oh blessed Trinity.

We adore you, one God: Father and Son and Holy
Spirit. Oh blessed Trinity.

Forgive us our sins, grant eternal life, give peace and
glory. Oh blessed Trinity.

Oh blessed and blessed and glorious Trinity: Father and
Son and Holy Spirit. Oh blessed Trinity.

Oh blessed, blessed, glorious unity of the Father, Son,
and Holy Spirit. Oh blessed Trinity.

Oh true, great, everlasting unity: Father, Son, and Holy
Spirit. Oh blessed Trinity.

Have mercy on us, have mercy on us, have mercy on us.
Oh blessed Trinity.

Praise to you, glory to you, gratitude to you forever and
ever. Amen.

48. Prayer for the Conversion of One's Father
John of Damascus (ca. 675–749) ☙ *20*

Oh Lord, with your gracious and merciful eye, look upon
the contrition of my heart. According to your certain promise, stay with me as I acknowledge you to be the maker and
defender of all creation. Cause a spring of water to rise up
within me; give words to me as I open my mouth and a mind
so set on you, the chief cornerstone, so that your unworthy
servant may be enabled to preach to my father, as I should,
the mystery of your plan of redemption, and remove him
by your power from the futile lies of wicked demons so that
I may deliver him to you, his God and Lord, who does not
desire the death of us sinners but waits for us to turn back
and repent so that you will be glorified for all time. Amen.

49. Prayer in the Midst of Pain
John of Damascus (ca. 675–749) ☙ *20*

With pain earth's joys are mingled,
Earth's glories will not stay,

And, feebler than a shadow,
Like dreams they fade away.
In one brief sudden moment
Death comes to take their place,
But to you we pray, Lord Jesu,
With your unclouded face,
And with your own sweet beauty,
You who have loved us best,
Look on him you have chosen,
And grant your servant rest.

Woe for the bitter struggle
That racks the parting soul!
Woe for the tears she pours
When none can make her whole!
She looks to the angels
But supplicates in vain;
Her hands to men she stretches,
But from there no help may gain.
Then mindful, dearest brethren,
How soon this life must cease,
Pray we to Christ for mercy,
And for our brother's peace.

Vain, vain are all possessions
That men may gather here;
They last for us no longer
When death is coming near.
Our wealth hath no abiding,
Fame may not with us go;
When death is hasting onward,
They vanish with their show.
And so to Christ Eternal
Cry we, of his dear grace,
To grant our brother quiet
In his glad dwelling place.

Where are the world's affections,
Where dream of earthly gain,
Where are the gold and silver,
And where the serving train?
All, all are dust and ashes,
All are but as a shade,
So to the King Eternal
Be our petition made.
Grant, Lord, your ceaseless blessings
To him now called away;

And give him joys unfading,

And rest that lasts always. Amen.

50. Prayer for Devotion to God

Anselm (1033/34–1109) 🍂 *21*

Oh God, I pray that I may so know you and love you that I might rejoice in you, and if I am not able in this life to do so fully, that I will make progress day after day until that joy becomes complete. Let the knowledge of you grow in me here, and there let it be complete. Let your love grow in me here, and there let it be complete, so that my joy here is great in hope, and my joy there is complete in reality.

Lord, through your Son you command, or rather, you counsel, us to ask, and you promise that we will receive, "that our joy may be full" (John 16:24). I ask, Lord, for what you counsel "through a wonderful counselor" (Isa. 9:6). Let me receive what you promise by your truth, "that my joy may be full" (John 16:24). True God, help me receive, "that my joy may be full" (John 16:24).

In the meantime, let my mind meditate on it. Let my tongue speak of it. Let my heart love it, my mouth proclaim it. Let all of me hunger for it, my flesh thirst for it, my whole substance long for it, until "I enter into the joy of my Lord" (Matt. 25:21), who is God, triune and one, "blessed forever. Amen" (Rom. 1:25).

51. Prayer to Strengthen Love for God
Anselm (1033/34–1109) ☙ *21*

Lord Jesus Christ, my Redeemer, my mercy, my salvation: I praise you and give you thanks, though even these gifts of thanks fail to live up to your goodness, which deserves far greater devotion. They are much too lean for the full beauty of your affection. Yet I will give some sort of praise, some sort of thanks. Though my thanks will not be what they should, I will give as much as my soul is able.

Hope of my heart, strength of my soul, helper of my weakness: Let your powerful kindness complete what I am trying to accomplish despite my tepid weakness. Oh my life, the end for which I aim even though I have not yet loved you as I should, please let my longing for you match what my love should be.

52. Prayer of Longing for God
Anselm (1033/34–1109) ☙ *21*

I implore you, Lord, for my heart is bitter with desolation; sweeten it with your comfort. I implore you, Lord, for when I began to seek you, I was hungry; let me not leave you empty. I have come to you famished; do not let me leave unsatisfied. I have come as a beggar goes to the wealthy, as one who is miserable to the one who gives mercy; please do not let me return penniless or despised. And if indeed, "before I eat, I sigh" (Job 3:24), let me eat even after I sigh.

Lord, I cannot help but look down when I am bent over. Please lift me so that I may look upward. "My iniquities have risen above my head." They have enveloped me, "and like a heavy burden" (Ps. 38:4), they weigh me down. Take this burden from me, set me free, "lest the pit close its mouth over me" (Ps. 69:15). Allow me to look up at your light, either from afar or from the depths. Teach me to seek you, and show yourself to me when I seek, for I cannot seek you unless you teach me, nor can I find you unless you show yourself to me.

Let me seek you by desiring you; let me desire you by seeking you. Let me find you by loving you; let me love you by finding you.

53. Prayer to the Holy Spirit
Anselm (1033/34–1109) ❧ *21*

Come, oh come, most gracious comforter of afflicted souls and helper in tribulations. Come, cleanser of sins and healer of wounds. Come, strengthener of the weak, comforter of the downtrodden. Come, teacher of the humble and destroyer of the proud. Come, devoted father of the orphans, gentle protector of widows. Come, hope of the poor, reviver of the sick. Come, star of the navigator, port of refuge for the shipwrecked. Come, singular glory of those who live, singular salvation of those who die.

Come, most Holy Spirit, come, and have mercy on me. Make me fit for you. And graciously reach down to me so that my insignificance may be pleasing to your greatness, my weakness to your strength, according to the multitude of your mercies through Jesus Christ my Savior who lives with the Father in unity and reigns forever and ever. Amen.

54. Prayer for Forgiveness
Anselm (1033/34–1109) ✿ *21*

Oh merciful God, indeed, the very author of mercy, it is your mercy that elicits this request. Forgive me all the offenses of my recklessness so that my soul may be filled with the sweetness of your kindness and may be granted the extravagant gift of a complete pardon. Whatever I have done adding to my own guilt, erase and wipe out all of it through your indescribable holiness. Do not let the mercy of your forgiveness be distant from me. Whatever I have taken on that is contrary to your will, whether through the deception of the devil or even through my own iniquity and weakness, I beg of you, in your piety and mercy, to cleanse me by your indulgence. Heal my wounds and forgive all my sins so that

I am no longer separated from you by my iniquities. Always and everywhere protected by your defenses, let me cling to you, Lord. Somehow let me grasp a share of the eternal glory you have prepared for those who care about you—the glory that the eye has not seen and the ear has not heard and that has not yet ascended into the heart of humanity. Amen.

55. Prayer for God to Hear My Prayer
Anselm (1033/34–1109) ❧ *21*

Hear me, oh Lord, oh great and good Lord. My soul hungers and longs to feed upon your love, but my soul cannot satisfy itself, for my heart cannot find the name to invoke that will be sufficient. No words make sense to me when my affection receives gifts from you. I have prayed, Lord, as much and as well as I could, but I long to do more.

Hear me, answer me as you are able, however you desire. I pray as a weak and sinful person. Hear me, answer me, you who are both mighty and merciful. And grant my prayer for my friends and the enemies for whom I have prayed, and, according to your good will and in accordance with your knowledge give to each your merciful healing, both to the living and the dead. Do not act merely as my heart desires nor as my mouth requests. Rather, act as you alone know and will so that I should desire and should ask, Savior of the world, who with the Father and the Holy Spirit lives and reigns as God for all time. Amen.

56. Prayer for God to Act in Mercy
Anselm (1033/34–1109) ❧ *21*

I know, oh Lord God, ruler of my life, that every great and perfect gift is from above, coming down from the Father, the fountain of lights (James 1:16). I know that I can offer nothing that is acceptable or pleasing to you unless I have first drawn it from the fountain of your goodness. And I can only do that if you first enlighten me and teach me. I know that the promise of your mercy must go before any of my efforts. I know, dearest Father, that if I cannot pilfer or steal your goodness from you, I surely cannot, by any merits of my own, figure out a way to return to you and please you. For what payments can my own merit earn but the punishment of eternal death? I know that it lies solely in your good pleasure to determine whether you will destroy me (as the great multitude of my evil deeds, my offenses, my acts of negligence, and even my failures to act deserve) or remake me, molding me into what is acceptable to you according to the inestimable riches of your mercy, for you alone, the only Creator, can remake what you have already made. Amen.

57. Prayer to Know Christ

Bonaventure (1221–1274) ☙ 22, quoting Anselm

I have not yet expressed or even begun to understand, oh Lord, just how great the rejoicing will be from your blessed ones. Of course, they will rejoice as much as they love, and their love will match their comprehension. But the question remains: How much of you will they be able to grasp and, thus, how much can they actually love you? In this life, no eye has seen, no ear has heard, nor has the heart of humanity even begun to grasp how well they will know you and, therefore, love you in the next life.

Oh God, I pray that I may know you and love you so that I may find my joy in you. If I am not able to know and love you completely in this life, at least allow me to make some progress every day until the moment of completion arrives. Let the knowledge of you so develop in me here in this life that there, in the next life, it may be complete. Let the love of you so grow here in this life that there, in the next life, it may be full. Here, let my joy be great in hope; there, let it be full in actuality.

Lord, through your Son, you have commanded us—no, you have counseled us—to ask, and you have promised to grant this request so that our joy may be full. Faithful God, I beg of you, please make my joy full. I ask, Lord, precisely as you have suggested through your wonderful counselor; I will receive what you have promised by your truth so that my joy may indeed be made full.

For now, let my mind meditate on this joy. Let my tongue speak of it. Let my heart love it exclusively. Let my conversation focus on it. Let my soul hunger for it. Let my flesh thirst for it. Let my whole being desire it until I finally enter the joy of my Lord, who is the triune and one God, blessed forever and ever. Amen.

58. Prayer for Understanding God
Bonaventure (1221–1274) ✥ *22*

Let us bow the knees of our heart in devotion before the throne of the eternal majesty. With tears and groans before the royal throne of the judicial Trinity, let us pray without ceasing that God the Father, by his blessed Son, would grant us the grace of mental acuity in the Holy Spirit, that we may know what is the breadth and length and depth and height, that by this we may attain to the final purpose of all our desires. Amen.

59. Prayer for Right Desires
Thomas Aquinas (1225–1274) ✥ *23*

Grant to me, oh merciful God, that I may wholeheartedly desire, prudently investigate, truthfully acknowledge, and perfectly fulfill all that is pleasing to you for the praise and glory of your name. Put my life in order and grant that I may know what you require of me. Allow me the ability to do what is necessary and fitting for my soul.

Grant to me, oh Lord my God, both in times of prosperity and in times of adversity, that I may not be unduly excited by wealth nor unduly depressed by hardships. Let me find joy in nothing except what leads to you. Let me find sorrow in nothing except what leads away from you. Let me desire to please no one but you; let me fear to displease no one but you.

Let me despise all that is temporary, oh Lord, and let me cherish all that is eternal. Make any joy that is not from you tiresome and unpleasant, and teach me to desire nothing that is apart from you. Oh Lord, let me delight in the work that is done for you, and let all rest that is not centered on you be wearisome to me.

Oh God, allow me to direct my heart to you that I may continually grieve my failures so that I may truly change.

Shape me, oh Lord my God, in such a way that I may be obedient without protest, poor without discouragement, pure without corruption, patient without complaint, humble without posturing, cheerful without foolishness, mature without undue gravity, agile without levity, fearing you without being in despair, truth filled without any hint of duplicity, good without presumption, able to correct my neighbor without pride, to edify my neighbor by word and example without pretense.

Grant me, oh Lord God, a vigilant heart so that no curious thought could distract me from you. Give me a noble heart that no unworthy desire could possibly debase. Give me a resolute heart that no evil intention could divert. Give me a firm heart that no tribulation could break. Give me a free heart that no ungodly desire could enslave.

Grant me, oh Lord my God, an understanding to know you, diligence to seek you, wisdom to find you, conversation to please you, perseverance to wait faithfully for you, and confidence finally to embrace you. Grant that I may receive your discipline here with a desire to change so that, by your grace, I may make good use of your gifts in this life. Thereby, let me enjoy your joys in the land of glory where you live and reign as God forever and ever. Amen.

60. Prayer for Students
Thomas Aquinas (1225–1274) ✎ *23*

Ineffable Creator, who, from the riches of your wisdom, designed three classes of angels and placed them above the heavens in a wonderful order and distributed the parts of the universe in the most elegant way, you who are the true source of light and wisdom, deign to shed upon my understanding a ray of your light to remove from me the double darkness of my birth, the darkness of both sin and ignorance.

You, who make the tongues of children speak eloquently and who infuse my lips with the grace of your blessing, give me a keen mind for understanding, a capacity to retain knowledge, a method and facility for learning, the subtlety of interpretation, and an abundant capacity for communication. Direct the beginning, oversee the progress, and bring the task to completion, you who are truly God and man, who lives and reigns forever and ever. Amen.

61. Prayer of Thanksgiving for God's Blessing
Thomas Aquinas (1225–1274) ✇ *23*

I praise, glorify, and bless you, my God, for the immeasurable goodness you have given to me, a completely unworthy recipient. I praise your mercy that you have granted to me for so long, your sweetness in disciplining me, your devotion in calling me, your kindness in accepting me, your mercy in forgiving my sins, your goodness that goes over and above what I could possibly deserve, your patience that does not record my wrongs, your humility that consoles me, your patience that protects me, your eternality that conserves me, your truth that rewards me.

My God, what can I say about your unspeakable generosity? For you call the fugitive home. You welcome the one who is returning. You help the one who falters. You cheer up the one who despairs. You encourage the negligent. You prepare the warrior for battle. You crown the victor. You do not reject a repentant sinner. You do not remember the wrongs he has done.

You free him from a multitude of dangers. You soften his heart for repentance. You use correction to teach him to fear. You allure him with promises. You discipline him with whips. You guard him with angelic ministers.

You enter our time to supply our needs, but you reserve eternity for us. You inspire with the sheer beauty of creation. You entice with redemptive mercy. You promise rewards as payment.

All the praises I can offer do not suffice. I thank your majesty for the abundance of your immeasurable goodness, and I ask that you would continue to multiply your grace in me, conserve what is multiplied, and reward what is conserved. Amen.

62. Prayer for Receiving God
Thomas Bradwardine (ca. 1290–1349) ❧ *24*

My God, I love you above all else, and I desire you as my ultimate end. I seek you for you alone and for nothing else, always and in all things, with my whole heart and strength, with crying and groaning, with constant labor and grief. What then will you finally provide for me? If you do not provide yourself, you provide nothing. If you do not give yourself to me, you give nothing. If I do not find you, I find nothing. Anything less than you would not be a reward by any means; rather, it would be a heavy affliction, for before I sought you, I hoped at length to find you and to hold on to you. By that delightful hope I was sweetly comforted in all my labors. But now, if you will deny yourself to me, whatever else you could give would leave my hope completely disappointed—not for a short time, but forever. I would languish with desire forever; I would weep with my languishing; I would sorrow in my mourning because I would ever remain empty and unsatisfied. Will I not grieve inconsolably, complain unceasingly, be frustrated interminably? This is not the way, oh best, most gracious, most loving God. It does not fit with your character. It does not match with who you have revealed yourself to be.

Grant to me, therefore, oh most blessed God, that I may love you for you alone and above everything else. Let me seek you in all things in this present life so that in the end I may find you and keep you forever in the life to come.

63. Prayer of the Humble Servant
Thomas à Kempis (1380–1471) ❧ *25*

Oh most sweet and loving Lord, whom I now desire to follow with all devotion, you know my weaknesses and the needs I face. You know the many sins and evils that oppressively weigh upon me, how often I am grieved, tempted, troubled, and defiled. I come to you for help; I crave comfort and support from you. I speak to you, for you know all things. You even know my inward thoughts, and you alone can perfectly comfort and help me. You know what good things I need most, and you know how lacking I am in virtue.

Behold, I stand before you poor and naked, calling for your grace and craving mercy. Refresh me, your hungry beggar. Inflame my cold heart with the fire of your love. Enlighten my blindness with the brightness of your presence. Turn all earthly things that would distract me from you into bitterness, all things dreadful and angry that would debase me into patience, all low and created things that would wrongly hold my attention into worthlessness and oblivion. Lift up my heart to you in heaven and do not allow me to wander upon earth. Let me be enthralled by you now and forevermore, for you alone are my meat and my drink, my love and my joy, my sweetness and all my good.

Oh, that with your presence you would light an all-consuming fire in me. Burn and conform me to yourself that I might be made one spirit with you by the grace of inward union with Christ and by the emboldening of impassioned love. Please do not let me leave you hungry or dry, but deal mercifully with me as you have so often dealt wonderfully with your people. What good is it if I am zealous for you and yet die from myself, since you are the fire that is always burning yet never destroys, the love that purifies the heart, and the enlightening that brings understanding?

64. Prayer for Hope
Thomas à Kempis (1380–1471) 🐟 *25*

Your eyes saw me even before I was formed. Oh Lord my God, what in the end will become of me, seeing that daily I offend you? When will I amend my life as I know I should? When will it be better with me? When will my strength be enough? When will I be able to overcome this weakness?

I am cast headlong into the deep pit of filthiness. How could I dare to hope that I will rise again, to change, to go forward, and to reach the finish line? Surely, in my own strength, I have no hope. Ah, that my hope in you was stronger! I am in immense despair because my weakness continues to grow through all of these constant troubles, and I see no end of my sorrow, no end of my sin.

I often say, "Today, I will start to change. Now is the time for me to do my best to change myself, starting right now." Alas, each time I make those commitments, sin stands before me. The enemy lifts himself up against me, and my wicked habits come at me with unbearable strength, fighting against my will to change.

O Lord, see how I am cast down and trodden underfoot: take note of the troubles I endure. Lift up your right hand and deliver me from my persecutors, for they are too strong for me. My wisdom is gone, and my strength has failed me. My arm is broken, and even if it weren't, my sword cannot save me.

I cannot find a protector anywhere, someone in whom I can seek refuge, someone who will welcome me and who can heal me. I know no one. You alone are capable of protecting me, but I am too ashamed to approach you because I know I have offended you.

I have sinned. Oh God, forgive me! I am sorry, so very sorry that I ever broke your commands. Do with me as you see fit, but be merciful.

You would be just in forsaking me and leaving me to the hands of my enemy. But Lord, remember me, your creation.

Revive what is decayed in me, for of its own accord, it cannot recover.

Take note of my groaning and my troubles. Never forget the pain and grief of my heart. Oh merciful Father, take note of my enslavement, my imprisonment. Open your eyes to the cruelty that I endure and free me from my chains, from the prison, and my wretched bondage.

Even if a person has a long life, does that necessarily mean he will get better? Who knows whether he will change for the better or for the worse? People simply do not know how they will grow or how they will wind up, and the idea that they will continue to mature is very doubtful because of the manifold evils and dangerous temptations.

Upon initial conversion from sin, many are good and humble, but afterward they become contrary and rebellious. They start out seeming modest and devout, zealous and silent, but in the end they prove to be careless and licentious babblers and even savage. Those who, at the beginning, were able to control their wicked affections, in the end often lose all care about either what they say or do. And so, little by little, wickedness takes root and increases if it is not prevented at the beginning.

Who can help but fear, then, and be concerned, seeing such evil overtakes the seemingly good and modest? Again, who actually knows whether he is of the elect or has the strength to endure such conditions?

We are all to be tested, and who can be certain that he will not be burned, seeing that temptation is a fire? Therefore, all should fear and yet hope for the better, but none should presume rashly nor proudly that he will be secure. Indeed the gold that has been tested will be preserved, but I advise you, oh man, to consider well what metal you are made of. The heavenly purger will purify; he will find the sons of Levi, all that are his servants.

Not everything that looks like gold is actually gold. Neither is it always stubble that is left after the harvest or false silver that endures the beating, for God sees the very thoughts and into the deep recesses of hearts, and in them he most commonly works his wonders, miracles that are often overlooked.

Oh Lord God, what joy can I have in this world when I think about the uncertainty and frailty of all things under heaven? Notwithstanding, this I know for certain: you are good, and your mercy reaches to multiple generations for those who fear you, for your infinite goodness and mercy is greater than all my sins. And this will be my comfort, even while you are patient with me as I continue to mature.

65. Prayer regarding the Miseries of This Life
Thomas à Kempis (1380–1471) ❧ *25*

Let me understand the shortness of my days. So long as I am in this world, I am wicked, and while I continue upon the earth, I am poor, a stranger, and a pilgrim. I brought nothing into the world, and I am certain I can take nothing when I leave, for naked I came out of my mother's womb, and naked I will return. As a shadow that fades away and as a feather that is tossed up and down with the wind, as a guest who only stays one night, so shall I suddenly pass away.

All the time we have in life is as the shortest night. Few and evil are my days, and after a little while they will end, and it will be as though they have never been. And when a man is dead, what is left but his filthiness? Who will have any care for a stinking carcass? Or who will inquire of those who are dead, whereas being alive, others did care for them?

For a little while a person may be remembered by his friends or by strangers, but assuredly the righteous will be remembered forever because they are linked to God for eternity, and God is always the same and will never die. Therefore, happy are those who do not place trust in humanity, nor find joy in any worldly thing, but instead fix their heart in heaven, for whatever is in this world is both temporary and empty.

Call to your mind those who have lived since the world began and please tell me where they are now. And those whom you see and hear that are living now, how long do you think they will last? Say, therefore, "Everyone that lives is but vanity."

Oh miserable and wretched life! Oh frail and lamentable life, which good men suffer rather than desire, and wicked men, although they desire it, cannot enjoy it for long! Oh vanity of this world, when will you have an end? When will you cease?

Yet the time will come when all the elect shall be set free from the bondage of corruption, though even now they mourn because they are estranged from the kingdom of Christ. I have a deep longing for the whole world to wither up in my heart. And I desire that you, my Lord God, even my immortal spouse, would seem sweet to my soul.

Undoubtedly, the fleeting joy of this present life is but a false and bitter potion. Let them drink of this desire, for afterward, they shall feel a most bitter disease. And the more one has drunk of it, the sharper his torments will be because the whole pleasure of this world will pass away more quickly than the wind and leave nothing but pain and burning.

Get out of my sight, oh deceitful glory of this world and all foolish pleasure of the flesh. You draw many in and you deceive, but in the end, you leave and destroy them. Woe to those who believe your lies. Woe to those who have drowned in them.

But come close to me most holy humility. Let me fully renounce the world's glamor. Never leave me, oh sweet remembrance of my present pilgrimage.

What am I but ashes and dust? And where am I headed but back to the earth? Oh, how wretched have I become! How right I am to lament when I think about my own journey.

If I live well and continue so, there is no reason I should fear an evil death. But who can glory in a good life and a pure conscience? He who knows himself to be such a person, let him rejoice in the Lord and take compassion on me, a sinner.

I have no desire to live because misery surrounds me on every side, but an evil conscience is afraid to die because it cannot answer God. When the prophet said, "My heart is prepared, oh God, my heart is prepared!" [Ps. 107:2], he clearly was not afraid. Oh Lord, the God of my salvation, let my life come to a good end, and do not prolong the days of my lamentation. With sorrow I came into this prison, and I will not get out without grief.

I often think this life is long—largely because of the continual misery and troubles I suffer. But in truth, it is not long, for it passes away swiftly. To a person who lives in pain and misery, all time is long, and a single day seems like a year. This makes my life tedious and troubles me even more as I consider all the miseries I face.

But if any consolations or joys appear, they force me to determine whether or not they are from God. If they are indeed from God, I accept them gladly, even though I do not know how long they will continue. No matter how short-lived they are, they please me well. But I deeply long for God to pour out those blessings upon me and cause them to stay with me for a long while! Yet, the joys and pleasures that are not of God are vile and fading even though they appear sweet and pleasant. Thus, this life passes away, continually replenished both with good and evil things.

Therefore, so long as I live in this world, I am but a poor pilgrim. I cannot truly say I have enough because presently I am lacking in the good, but the good that I am looking for I have discovered is you, in whom I believe. When your glory has appeared and replenished me, then, even then, I will acknowledge that I have enough.

In the meantime, because this word is hidden from me, much grief and sorrow envelop my soul. Therefore, remembering your holy saying, I often repeat this to myself: "My soul is very heavy, even until death" [Matt. 26:38]. It would be well for me if the hour would come when neither grief nor sorrow did possess me! But Lord, considering this, I beg of you, let your goodness protect and preserve me!

3

Reformation Church
(1500–1700)

66. Prayer to Be Filled by God
Martin Luther (1483–1546) ❧ *26*

Behold, Lord, I am an empty vessel that needs to be filled. Oh Lord, fill me. I am weak in the faith; strengthen me. I am cold in love; warm me to the point of zeal so that my love may reach my neighbor. I do not have a steadfast belief. I suffer from doubt, and I am unable to trust completely. Oh Lord, help me. Increase my faith and strengthen my trust. All my good treasure is stored in you. I am poor; you are rich. And you came to be merciful to the poor. I am a sinner; you are just. With me is an abundance of sin, but with you is the fullness of justice. And thus I will say, "I want to have you from whom I can receive everything, but to whom I can give nothing."

67. Prayer for Perseverance in Holiness
Martin Luther (1483–1546) ✎ *26*

Oh my dear Lord Jesus Christ, you know the poor condition of my soul and my great ailments. I lament to you alone with an open heart. Unfortunately, I find that I do not have the will and resolution that I should and fall daily as a sick, sinful human. You know that I long to have that will and resolution, but my enemy strikes and takes me captive. Deliver this poor sinner, according to your godly will, from all evil and temptations. Develop and strengthen me in true Christian faith. Give me mercy to love my neighbors faithfully with all my heart and as myself. Let me love them as brothers.

Give me patience and long-suffering in all persecution and troubles. You told Peter that he should not only forgive seven times, and you have told us to seek consolation from you. So, I come to you with the assurance of your promise, and I turn to you as the true pastor and bishop of my soul for all my needs. You are the only one who knows when and how to help me. Your will be done, and your name be praised forever. Amen.

68. Prayer for Repentance
Martin Bucer (1491–1551) ✹ *27*

Oh Lord God and heavenly Father, you are a just judge to punish everyone who continues to offend you, as you are a gracious Father to receive everyone who seeks to please you into your mercy. Show me your grace and favor so that I may truly learn to hate my sins. Instead of lulling myself to sleep in sin, let me be so cast down in heart that I may confess with my mouth the honor, glory, and praise due to your holy name. In your great mercy you instruct us by your holy word. For your name's sake, then, allow your instruction to so lighten and clear our conscience that in due examination of all our holy life we may truly learn to be angry and displeased with all our former and corrupt living.

Please draw near to us and guide our footsteps in the true and perfect way of obedience to your holy laws and commandments. Send your holy angel to protect us; the enemy's infernal army can never prevail against us. With strong faith in Jesus Christ, we may withstand all the crafty engines and snares of the evil one, knowing undoubtedly that you never forsake those who put their trust in you.

Let us not be led by the infirmity of our sinful flesh, but strengthen us by the Holy Spirit. Do not let us remain under your wrath and vengeance through hypocrisy. Rather, so change us that we may, without ceasing, sigh and groan unto you with true and unfeigned repentance. Even if we are not always prone to ask and pray as we should, even so, good Lord, for the sake of your name, stretch out your mighty hand so that by the gracious working of your Holy Spirit, our minds and hearts may be drawn away from all earthly and corruptible things. Allow our prayers to come from a deep, authentic affection so that we never presume to come before you with a double heart, knowing that if we do not ask in faith, we cannot obtain anything from you. Therefore, increase our faith, oh merciful Father, that we may presently live in the benefit of remission and pardon of all our sins, through the merits and death of Christ Jesus our Savior. Hereafter, work in us forever to live in the righteous fear of you and to stand in awe of your displeasure toward sin so that you may continue as our merciful Father, world without end. God, please grant this.

69. Prayer for Divine Defense
Thomas Cranmer (1489–1556) ❧ *28*

Almighty God, give us grace that we may cast away the works of darkness. Place upon us the armor of light now, while we have mortality (the same mortal life that your Son took on in great humility), so that in the last day, when he comes again in his glorious majesty to judge both the quick and the dead, we may rise to immortal life through him who lives and reigns with you and the Holy Spirit, now and forever. Amen.

70. Prayer for the Reading of Scripture
Thomas Cranmer (1489–1556) ❧ *28*

Blessed Lord, who has caused all Holy Scriptures to be written for our learning, allow us to hear them, read them, mark them, learn them, and inwardly digest them in such a way that, by the patience and comfort of your holy word, we may embrace and ever hold on to the blessed hope of everlasting life that you have given to us in our Savior, Jesus Christ.

71. Prayer for the Mundane
John Calvin (1509–1564) ❧ *29*

My God, my Father and Preserver, in your goodness, you have watched over me during the night and brought me to this day. Please now grant that I may spend it wholly in the worship and service of your most holy deity. Let me not think or say or do a single thing that is not rightly in your service or in submission to your will so that all of my actions may aim at your glory and the salvation of my neighbor and that even the example of my life may lead others to serve you. Just as you use the rays of the sun to provide light to this world so that life may exist, so also enlighten my mind by the radiance of your Spirit, that he may guide me in the way of your righteousness. Let my sole purpose—for everything I set my mind to—be your honor and service. Let me seek happiness solely from your grace and goodness. Let me not attempt anything whatsoever that is not pleasing to you.

Grant also that even while I perform the mundane duties of this life (providing basic necessities for myself like food and clothing), I may set my mind on things above to the blessed and heavenly life that you have promised your children. As the protector of both my soul and my body, please strengthen and fortify me against all the attacks of the devil and deliver me from all the dangers that are constant in this life. But seeing that beginning the journey is simple compared to the perseverance required for completing it, I, therefore, beg of you, oh Lord, that you would not only be my guide and director today but that you would also oversee the entirety of my journey. As I should continue to grow, please add daily to your gifts of grace until I fully conform to your Son Jesus Christ, whom we justly regard as the true sun, shining constantly in our minds.

In order that I can obtain these great blessings, act according to your infinite mercy. Forget and forgive my many offenses, as you have promised that you will do for those who call upon you in sincerity. Grant that I may hear your voice in the morning since I have placed my hope in you. Show me the way to walk since I have lifted my soul to you. Deliver me from my enemies, oh Lord, since I have fled to you. Teach me to do your will, for you are my God. Let your good Spirit guide me into the land of righteousness.

72. Prayer for Study
John Calvin (1509–1564) ❧ *29*

Oh Lord, fountain of all wisdom and learning, since out of your special goodness you have allowed me to receive an education in my youth that will help me to honest and holy living, please also grant through the enlightening of my mind (which otherwise labors in blindness) that I may be able to acquire knowledge. Strengthen my memory so that I may retain what I have learned. Govern my heart so that I may be willing and even eager to learn, so that I do not miss out on the opportunity you have provided because of my own laziness. May it please you for your Spirit to dwell in me, the Spirit of understanding, truth, judgment, and prudence, for without your Spirit, my study will have no value and my entire education will be in vain.

In all of my study, regardless of the focus, help me understand its proper place and role in my life, namely, that it would allow me know you in Christ Jesus, your Son. May everything that I learn assist me to observe the right rule of godliness. You have promised to bestow wisdom even on children and especially on those who are humble. You have promised to give the knowledge of yourself to those who are upright in heart. Yet you declare that you will humble the wicked and the proud so that they will fade away. Therefore, I beg of you that you would be pleased to turn me to true humility that I may be teachable and obedient first of all to you and then to those who are rightly in positions of authority over me.

Please get rid of all vicious desires from my heart and replace them with an earnest desire to seek you. Finally, let my only purpose be to qualify myself in this earthly life so that when I grow up I may serve you in whatever position you would assign to me. Amen.

73. Prayer for Unity in the Faith
John Calvin (1509–1564) ❧ *29*

Almighty God, since at the coming of Christ, your Son, you really did what your servants, the prophets, had previously foretold, and since you invite us daily to the unity of faith so that with a unified effort we may truly serve you, grant that we may not continue in disunity, everyone pursuing their own perverse inclinations at a time when Christ is gathering us to you. Nor let us only profess with our mouths, only in words, that we are under your government, but let us prove that we believe this with real sincerity. And may we then add brotherly love for each other to the true and lawful worship of your name so that, with those united efforts, we may promote each other's good and so that our adoption may be proven and be constantly reconfirmed. May we always be able to call on you as our Father with full confidence through Christ, our Lord. Amen.

74. Prayer for Christian Growth
John Calvin (1509–1564) ❧ *29*

Almighty God, since we have already entered in hope upon the threshold of our eternal inheritance, and since we know that there is a mansion for us in heaven because Christ, our head and the firstfruits of our salvation, has been received there, grant that we may proceed more and more in the way of your holy calling until at length we reach the goal and so enjoy that eternal glory of which you give us a taste in this world by the same Christ, our Lord. Amen.

75. Prayer for a Quiet Mind
Henry Bull (d. ca. 1577) ❧ *30*

There is nothing, oh Lord, more like your holy nature than a quiet mind. You have called us out of the troublesome noise of the world into your quiet rest and peace, which the world cannot give—the peace that passes all understanding. Houses are prepared for us so that we can be safe from the weather, from the cruelty of beasts, from the noise of people, and for rest from the toils of the world. Oh gracious Father, grant that, through your great mercy, my body may enter into this proverbial house of rest from outward actions so that it may become compliant and obedient to my soul and so that it will not resist righteous actions. Please allow that, in soul and body, I may have a godly quietness and peace to praise your holy name. Amen.

76. Prayer for Divine Assistance
Henry Bull (d. ca. 1577) ❧ *30*

You know, oh Lord, what is most profitable and expedient for me. Therefore, do with me in all things as it seems best to you, for, despite the way things might seem to me, what is best for me is that you do whatever is most just and blessed according to your godly wisdom. Thus, whether it be by prosperity or adversity, loss or gain, sickness or health, life or death, your will be done.

Cast out of my heart all unprofitable cares of worldly things. Suffer me not to be led with the unstable desires of earthly vanities. Rather, give me grace that all worldly and carnal affections may be mortified and may die in me.

Grant unto me the strength of your Holy Spirit to subdue this body of sin with the whole lusts thereof so that it might be obedient both in will, in mind, and in members—that it might do your holy will.

Assist me with your grace, oh Lord, so that I may be strengthened internally and be armed with your holy armor— the breastplate of righteousness, the shield of faith, the hope of salvation for a helmet, and the sword of the Spirit, which is your holy word. With that I may stand perfect in all that is your will and be found worthy through Christ to receive the crown of life that you have promised to all them who love you.

Give me grace that I may esteem all things in this world as they are, temporary and soon vanishing away, and let me see myself also with them drawing toward my end, for nothing under the sun may long abide, but all is vanity and affliction of spirit.

77. Prayer for God's Grace
Lancelot Andrewes (1555–1626) ❧ *31*

Give me grace, oh Lord, to remember my life's end (Deut. 32), to bruise the serpent's head (Gen. 3), to flee from opportunities to sin, to covenant with my senses so that I remain self-controlled (2 Cor. 11), to prevent scandals (Job 31), to discipline my body (Ezek. 14), to not sit idly (1 Cor. 9), to avoid keeping wicked company (Matt. 24), to maintain righteous friendships (Ps. 26), and to make personal prayer a priority (1 Cor. 7).

Oh Lord, hedge my way with thorns so that I may not even be able to find a path to vanity (Hos. 2). Rein me in with bit and bridle when I try to stray from you (Ps. 32). Oh Lord, compel me to come to you if mere request does not suffice.

78. Prayer for Deliverance
Lancelot Andrewes (1555–1626) ❧ *31*

From all innovations, private interpretations, minor differences in doctrine, contending about vanity and fruitless questions, endless disputations and controversies; from heresies both public and private; from schisms; from scandals; from the pernicious flattering of those with power (Acts 12); from the partiality of Saul (1 Sam. 14); from the contempt of Michal

(2 Sam. 6); from the priesthood of Micah (Judges 17); from the flesh hook of Hophni (1 Sam. 2); from being counted among the compatriots of Simon Magus (Acts 8) and Judas Iscariot (Matt. 26); from those who have a corrupt mind, unstable and unteachable (1 Tim. 6; 2 Pet. 3); from the arrogance of young scholars (1 Tim. 3); and from the people who contradict their minister when he is speaking according to the word of God, be merciful good Lord and deliver us (Hos. 4).

79. Prayer for Stewarding Wealth
George Webbe (1581–1642) ❧ *32*

Oh Lord God, who is infinite in greatness, power, glory, and majesty, all that is in heaven or on earth is yours. Yours is the kingdom, oh Lord, and you are exalted over all. Both riches and honor come from you. In your hand is power and might. In your hand is the ability to make great and to give strength to all.

Blessed be your holy name for all your mercies that from time to time you have given to me, your most unworthy servant—in particular, for that large and ample portion of these your earthly blessings that you have given to me instead of to others of your servants. By those blessings, I am better enabled to serve you and to set forth your glory, for what am I, or what is there in me, that your hand has been so bountiful to me? I acknowledge that it was not anything I deserve, nor was it my labor, my wit, nor my industry that has procured this wealth and riches for me. Rather, it was only your favor and mercy toward me.

Now therefore, oh my God, I thank you and praise your glorious name for this my blessing. I humbly beg of your divine majesty that your inward blessing may accompany these, your outward blessings. Sanctify them, good Lord, unto me, and sanctify me unto yourself so that I may use these blessings from you correctly and so that I may be found a faithful steward of what you have committed to my charge. Assist me with your grace that I may not overvalue this wealth above its worth. Let my heart not be set upon it; neither let it withdraw my heart from you. Preserve and keep me from pride, security, ungratefulness, covetousness, greediness, slothfulness, and negligence in the duties of your service, together with all other temptations, snares, and foolish lusts that commonly accompany worldly wealth and riches. Let not my prosperity puff me up nor choke the seed of your word nor impoverish spiritual graces in me. Let them not infatuate my understanding nor make me blind in the way to heaven. Let them not breed in me impenitence and hardness of heart nor expose me to your heavy wrath and judgments. Deliver me from the many cares, fears, sorrows, and manifold dangers that accompany riches. And forasmuch as by the addition of these temporal things you have given to me a double portion, so, good Lord, assist me with your grace that I may double my dutiful diligence in your service.

Give me grace evermore and in all things so that I may keep a good conscience. Make your blessings to me instruments and means of well-doing. Let me use this world as though I did not use it at all. Give me only the comfort in these earthly goods that you give to those who fear you. Continue and so increase my store (if it is your blessed will) that I may have enough for my family and that I may lay up some for my posterity, but also that I may have enough to give to those who are in need. Give me trite contentment in what you give me, and make me willing to leave all my wealth and riches behind whenever it pleases you to take them from me. Oh, let me not misspend the wealth that you have given to me in excessive, vain, or worldly living or keep it all to myself as if it were mine, but as a good and faithful steward, let me employ these riches to your honor, my master, and to the good of my fellow servants. Grant, oh heavenly Father, that I may so use these temporal things that I will not finally lose the eternal things.

Give me grace evermore truly to serve, glorify, and honor you and to put my trust in you, the living God, who gives us richly all things to enjoy, so that I may do good and be rich in good works, ready to distribute and willing to communicate, laying up in store for myself a good foundation against the time to come so that I may lay hold of eternal life. To that end, I beg of you to bring me, through the merits of your dear Son, to my blessed Savior Jesus Christ, to whom, with you and your Holy Spirit, be ascribed all honor and glory, praise, power, might, and dominion now and forevermore. Amen.

80. Prayer for Open Hands
Jeremy Taylor (1613–1667) ❧ *33*

You have called me to open my hand so that you can fill it. But I would not open my hand. I held the world tightly and kept my hand shut. I would not let it go. But please God, open my hand for me. And do not only open my hand, but also open my mouth—and not only my mouth, but my heart also. Grant that I may know nothing but you, that I may count everything as loss compared to you, and that I may strive to be conformed to you.

81. Prayer for Intimacy with Christ
Jeremy Taylor (1613–1667) ❧ *33*

Eternal God, sweetest Jesus, who received Judas with the affection of a savior, even allowed him to kiss your cheek, and did it with the serenity and tranquility of God, you also permitted the soldiers to bind you with an exemplary patience to all ages of martyrs. You even cured the wound of your enemy with the love of a parent and the tenderness of an infinite pity. Oh, kiss me with the kisses of your mouth, embrace me with the gifts of a gracious lord, and let my soul dwell and feast on you, the repository of eternal sweetness and refreshments. Bind me, oh Lord, with those bonds that held you fast, the chains of love. Allow that holy union to dissolve the cords of vanity and confine the bold pretensions of usurping passions. Imprison all the extravagancies of an impertinent spirit and lead sin captive to the dominion of grace and sanctified reason so that I may imitate all the parts of your holy passion. Allow me by your chains to get my freedom. By your kiss, enkindle love. By the touch of your hand and the breath of your mouth, cure all my wounds and restore the integrity of a holy penitent one and the purities of innocence so that I may love you and please you and live with you forever, oh holy and sweetest Jesus. Amen.

82. Prayer for Godly Desires
Jeremy Taylor (1613–1667) ❧ *33*

Fix my thoughts, my hopes, and my desires upon heaven and heavenly things. Teach me to despise the world, to repent deeply for my sins. Give me holy purposes to change me and spiritual strength and assistance to faithfully perform whatever I have righteously intended. Enrich my understanding with an eternal treasure of divine truths so that I may know your will. And you who work in us to will and to do your good pleasure, teach me to obey all your commandments and believe all your revelations, and make me a recipient of all your gracious promises.

83. Prayer for Protection from Temptations
Jeremy Taylor (1613–1667) ❧ *33*

Teach me to watch over all my ways so that I may never be surprised by sudden temptations or a careless spirit, nor ever return to folly and vanity. Set a watch, oh Lord, before my mouth, and keep the door of my lips so that my tongue would not offend either against piety or love. Teach me to think of nothing but you, oh God, and those things that align with your glory and your service. Teach me to speak nothing but you and your glories. Teach me to do nothing but what is fitting for your servant who has been sealed for the day of redemption by your infinite mercy in the graces of the Holy Spirit.

84. Prayer for Holy Living
Jeremy Taylor (1613–1667) ❧ *33*

Let no riches ever allow me to forget who I am. Let no poverty ever allow me to forget you. Let no hope or fear, no pleasure or pain, no external event, no internal weakness hinder or disrupt my obedience or turn me away from your commandments. Let your Spirit dwell with me forever, and make my soul just and charitable, full of honesty, full of religion, resolute and stable in holiness, and inflexible toward evil. Make me humble and obedient, peaceable and pious. Let me never envy anyone's good nor rightly deserve to be despised by others. And if I am so despised, teach me to bear it with meekness and charity.

85. Prayer for Marriage
Jeremy Taylor (1613–1667) ❧ *33*

Oh eternal and gracious Father, you have set marriage apart as a holy mystery, a representation of the union of Christ with his church. Please let the Holy Spirit guide me in my life as a spouse that it may not become a sin to me, and do not let the liberties that you have righteously given by the holy Jesus become an occasion of licentiousness for my own weakness and sensuality. Please forgive all those irregularities and overly sensual applications that may, in some degree or other, upset my spirit or hinder my maturity as a Christian. Let me in all experiences and circumstances be serious about my service for you. Let me be affectionate and loving to my spouse, a guide and good example for my family, and in all quietness, sobriety, prudence, and peace, a follower of those holy couples who have served you with godliness and a good testimony.

Please let the blessings of the eternal God, the blessings of the right hand and of the left, be upon the body and soul of your servant, my spouse, and let those blessings remain there until we have come to the end of a holy and happy life. Please grant that both of us may live forever in the embrace of the holy and eternal Jesus, our Lord and Savior. Amen.

86. Prayer for Help during Temptations
Jeremy Taylor (1613–1667) ✒ *33*

Oh Lord God of infinite mercy and infinite excellence, who has sent your holy Son into the world to redeem us from an intolerable misery, teach us a holy religion and forgive us an infinite debt. Give me your Holy Spirit so that my understanding and all my faculties may be so resigned to the discipline and doctrine of my Lord that I may be prepared in both mind and will to die for the testimony of Jesus and to suffer any affliction or tragedy that will possibly hinder my duty or tempt me to shame or to sin or to apostatize.

Let my faith produce in me a good life and a strong shield to repel the fiery darts of the devil, and let this faith be the author of a holy hope, of modest desires, of confidence in God, and of a never-failing love of you my God and of all the world so that I may never have my portion with unbelievers or uncharitable and desperate persons. Rather, let me be supported by the strengths of faith against all temptations. Let me be refreshed with the comforts of a holy hope in all my sorrows, and let me bear the burden of the Lord and the infirmities of my neighbor by the support of true love. Let the yoke of Jesus become easy to me so that my love may do all the miracles of grace. Let that love grow from grace to glory, from earth to heaven, from duty to reward, from the imperfections of a beginning and small, growing love to arrive at the consummation of an eternal and never-ending love. Do this, we pray, through Jesus Christ the Son of your love, the anchor of our hope, and the author and finisher of our faith. To him, with you, oh Lord God, Father of heaven and earth, and with your Holy Spirit, be all glory and love and obedience and dominion now and forever. Amen.

87. Prayer for Divine Pity
Jeremy Taylor (1613–1667) ✢ *33*

Oh eternal God, Father of mercies and God of all comfort, look upon the sadness and sorrows of your servant with much mercy. My sins lie heavy on me and press me greatly. There is no health left in my bones because of your displeasure and my sin. The waters have overtaken me, and I am stuck in the deep mire. My miseries remain without comfort because they are the just rewards of my sin. I am such an evil and unworthy person that though I have great desires, I have no disposition or worthiness to receive comfort. My sins have caused my sorrow, but my sorrow does not cure my sins. Unless for your own sake, and merely because you are good, you choose to have pity on me and relieve me, I am without remedy, just as now I have no comfort. Lord, pity me.

Lord, let your grace refresh my spirit. Let your comforts support me and your mercy pardon me, and never let my portion be among the hopeless and accursed spirits. You are good and gracious, and I throw myself upon your mercy. Let me never lose my grip on you, and do with me as seems good in your eyes. I cannot suffer more than I deserve, and yet I can need no relief so great that your mercy is not greater, for you are infinitely more merciful than I can be miserable. Your mercy, which is above all your works, is far above all my sin and all my misery. Dearest Jesus, let me trust in you forever, and let me never be confounded. Amen.

88. Prayer for Christian Unity
Jeremy Taylor (1613–1667) ✺ *33*

Oh holy Jesus, King of the saints and Prince of the universal church, preserve your spouse whom you have purchased with your right hand and redeemed and cleansed with your blood, the whole global church from one end of the earth to the other. She is founded upon a rock, but she is planted in the sea. Please keep her safe from schism, from heresy, and from sacrilege. Unite all her members with the bands of faith, hope, and love, and a visible communion when it seems good in your eyes. Let the daily sacrifice of prayer and thanksgiving never cease, but let it be forever presented to you, united to the intercession of our dearest Lord. And let it be successful in obtaining for every one of its members both grace and blessing, pardon and salvation. Amen.

89. Prayer for Sanctification

Henry Scougal (1650–1678) ✎ *34*

Most gracious God, Father and fountain of mercy and goodness, who has blessed us with the knowledge of our salvation and the way that leads to it: Make our hearts excited with the pursuit of that knowledge and that way because many things endeavor to distract us.

Let us not presume on our own strength or resist your divine assistance. While we are working to confirm our salvation diligently, teach us to depend on you for success. Open our eyes, oh God, and teach us from your law. Bless us with a diligent and tender sense of duty to it and a knowledge to discern things contrary to it. Direct us to keep your statutes so that we are not ashamed when we examine whether we have kept your commandments.

Fill our thoughts with a robust and holy disdain for the trivial entertainment with which the world attempts to allure us. Fill them to an extent that the strife would not be able to cloud our judgment or betray us to sin. Turn our eyes away from desiring worthless things, and make us alive in your law. Fill our souls with such a deep sense and full persuasion of the gospel truth that you revealed that it would regulate our lives, especially our interactions with others. Fill us so that the life we live in the flesh we would live through faith in the Son of God.

Oh, that the infinite perfections of your blessed nature and the astonishing expressions of your goodness and love would conquer and overpower our hearts! That our thoughts would be constantly rising toward you like flames of devout affection and would increase in sincere and active love toward all the world, for your sake! That we would wash away all filthiness of flesh and spirit, perfecting holiness in reverence, without which we can never hope to behold and enjoy you!

Finally, O God, grant that consideration of what you are compared to what we are in order to keep us both humble and meek before you, but also stir in us the strongest and most ardent aspirations toward you. We resign and give ourselves to the direction of your Holy Spirit. Lead us in your truth, and teach us, for you are the God of our salvation. Guide us with your wisdom. And then, receive us in your glory, to the credit and because of the intercession of your blessed Son, our Savior. Amen.

90. Prayer for Divine Protection of the Heart
John Kettlewell (1653–1695) ❧ *35*

I give you my heart, and I humbly pray that you would always keep it in your hands, since it is so unfaithful in loving what is good. When it is in my control, it is prone to follow all sorts of evils. Oh Father, keep my heart steadfast and unalterable in your ways. Let it not be inclined to any evil thing nor lean toward any of my former vanities. Keep my eyes from looking upon and my ears from listening to any sort of wickedness. Do not let my lips utter anything that is ungodly or my feet move even a step in any of the paths of death, but hold my whole spirit, soul, and body in a righteous fear of you. Keep me comfortable in the hope of your favor, through Jesus Christ, my blessed Lord and only Savior. Amen.

91. Prayer for Divine Peace
John Kettlewell (1653–1695) ❧ *35*

Let me have your peace, oh gracious Father! Comfort my trembling and broken heart with your hope. Cause me to hear the voice of joy and gladness, and revive me with the assurance of your love. Oh that I may be able—from my own experience—to speak great things of your readiness, to receive and comfort returning sinners and thereby draw others who are still running away from you back to your service.

Oh, that by seeing your goodness upon me, everyone that is godly may seek you in their distress and find mercy just as I have! But Lord, having found your mercy to poor sinners, let me not abuse it or presume upon it. Let me not repeat my sins simply because you are ready and willing to grant forgiveness. When you have spoken comfortably to me, make me careful to sin no more (lest a worse thing comes to me) but rather continue in holy and thankful obedience to you and never more to return to folly. Let the sense of your mercies, oh my God, serve no other use in me but to encourage my repentance and to support me in my fear of you until I come at length to enjoy your eternal favor through Jesus Christ my Lord, Amen.

4

Modern Church (1700–1900)

92. Prayer for the Morning

Isaac Watts (1674–1748) ✺ *36*

[Invocation and Adoration]

Oh Lord God who is most high and most holy, the creator, ruler, and judge of all mankind, I adore your majesty and worship you with humble reverence because you are infinitely wise, powerful, and gracious, far beyond our highest thoughts and above all of our praises. You have made the daylight for comings and goings of life and have woken me from sleep to see another morning in your comfort.

[Confession]

I acknowledge before you that I am utterly unworthy to come into your holy presence because my body is frail and humble and my sins have made me viler than mangy, rabid dogs. By nature, I am unholy and unclean. Moreover, even though my life has been short compared to eternity, my sins are many. In fact, the transgressions I commit daily testify against me, and they deserve destruction from your just hand. These transgressions are such that I cannot pretend to have merit to stand before your throne even now. But there is forgiveness with you, so that sinners will be encouraged to return to you with hope and love.

[Petitions for yourself]

Let your mercy, God, blot out all my offenses on account of the sufferings of your beloved Son. Let a sinful creature like me find favor in your sight because of his complete obedience and bloody death.

Pity me, heavenly Father, because of my natural blindness and ignorance. Instruct me by your word and your good Spirit so that I may know myself more—my own wants and weaknesses—that I may know you better as I discover your grace. Teach me the precepts of your law so that I can learn my duty to you. Let me grow daily in my humble acquaintance with Christ Jesus, who is the righteousness and strength and life of his people.

Work in my heart sincere repentance for all my past offenses, let my faith in Jesus be of the kind you approve, and draw my heart nearer to you in holy love. Let my faith produce the good fruits of obedience in the whole course of my life. I commit myself into his hands as my only and all-sufficient Savior so that he will deliver me both from sin and from hell and bring me safely into his heavenly kingdom.

Form my soul, oh Lord, to be like your holy image, which was lost by the sin of my first parents, Adam and Eve. Make right all of the irregular inclinations that are within me. Keep me from the powers of unruly appetites and from sudden and ungovernable passions of every kind. Help me to watch over my senses and my wandering heart at all times. Suppress all of the undue resentments I hold against who or what may injure me physically, mentally, emotionally, or spiritually. Instead, work a meek and serene temperament within me just like the one in my blessed Savior. I long to be like him and imitate his holy pattern. Kindle in my soul a pious flame of love to God and neighbors. Do so that my delight would be to do good to all, even those who have hurt me. But make me have a special love for my fellow Christians, those who bear your image and love Jesus your Son, whatever our differences, coalitions, or factions may be.

When you feel the need to correct me, oh my God, let it be done in measure and mercy. Let the fruit and effect of your correction take away my sins and make me partake in your holiness.

[Resignation]

I resign myself up entirely to whatever you want and deem wise according to the covenant of your grace. I desire to be yours in life and death and in the world to come forever.

[Petition for others]

I do not want to pray for myself only but for all people, as you have taught me. Shine the light of your gospel over the whole heart. Deliver those who are persecuted for righteousness's sake from the hands of those who hate them. Let the spirit of persecution be rooted out from the nations. When will the time come, Lord, that the freedom to worship you and the power of your gospel will be asserted and vindicated by the rulers of this world? When will it be that the governments of this earth will advance true faith with all their resources?

Maintain your gospel in its power and glory. Let the ministry of your word be accompanied by a demonstrable power of your Spirit so that the church on earth would be enlarged daily. Do so that the knowledge of you and of holiness would increase and abound among all people.

Look down in mercy on my dear family members and friends. Bless my parents, siblings, and family with all the gifts they need according to your providence and grace. Show your love to those who love me and enable me to forgive any who have hurt me. Let them repent of their sins, oh Lord, and partake of your forgiveness.

[Thanksgiving]

In Christ's name, I humbly thank you for all of your kindnesses that I enjoy and for all the hopes I have. I owe you alone, God, my very life and being, my health and comfort, and the use of my mind and body. You give me safety in the night and blessings in the morning. I receive from you all blessings of daily food, clothing, shelter, and the supports of nature, along with all your rich promises of grace and eternal salvation. Therefore, I pay all honor and praise to you alone.

[Blessing]

May the name of God my Father, my Savior, and my Sanctifier be glorified throughout everlasting ages. Amen.

93. Prayer from a Heart Broken by Grief
Samuel Johnson (1709–1784) ❧ *37*

Almighty and most merciful Father, you who sees all of our misery and knows our limitations, look down upon me and pity me. Defend me from violent intrusive thoughts and fortify in me the needed determination conducive to carrying out the duties that your providence has ordained. Also help me, through your Holy Spirit, by surely fixing my heart where true joys are to be found so that I may serve you with pure affection and a cheerful mind.

Have mercy on me, oh God, have mercy on me. Age and weakness oppress me; terror and anxiety surround me. Have mercy on me, my Creator and my Judge.

In all dangers protect me and in all distress relieve and free me. Help me by your Holy Spirit to an extent that I may now commemorate the death of your Son, our Savior Jesus Christ, in order that when this short and painful life will end, I will for his sake be received by him in eternal peace. Amen.

94. Prayer in the Evening
John Wesley (1703–1791) ❧ *38*

Almighty and most merciful Father, you are the one in whom we live, move, and have our being. We owe yesterday's safety and all of the comforts of this life to your tender compassion. We praise you, oh Lord. We bow our hearts before you, acknowledging that we have nothing other than what you have given us. "We give thanks to you, O God," who daily pours out your benefits on us [Ps. 75:1].

We bless you for your good gift of our health, for our food and clothing, for all our blessings in this life, and our desire to attain that life that is immortal.

We bless you for your love for us, which we feel moving our hearts toward you. Look at us, Lord—we present ourselves to you, to be exceedingly inspired by your love. We hope it moves us toward greater earnestness, zeal, and diligence in our duty to love God and neighbor. We desperately ask you to renew in us the vivid picture of you in all your righteousness, purity, mercy, faithfulness, and truth. Oh that Jesus, the hope of glory, may be formed in us in all humility, meekness, patience, and an absolute surrender of our souls and bodies to your holy will. We ask that this would be true of us: that we no longer live but that Christ lives in us, so that each of us could say, "the life I now live in the flesh I live by faith in the Son of God, who loved me and gave himself for me" [Gal. 2:20].

May we remember Jesus's love—he offered himself for our sins—more dearly and preciously. Let that sacrificial love continue to move us to offer ourselves to you and do your will, just as our blessed Master, Jesus, did. May we place all of our confidence in you, God, and trust ourselves with you, who has not even spared your "own Son but gave him up for us all" [Rom. 8:32]. May we humbly accept whatever circumstances you send to us, giving thanks for it all. We can be sure that you "will never leave us nor forsake us" [Heb. 13:5]. Guide us safely through all the changes of this life with an unchangeable love for you and a vivid sense of your love for us until we come to live with you and enjoy you forever.

Now that we are laying down to sleep, take us into your gracious protection. Settle our minds and hearts with the quiet and delightful thought of our Lord Jesus's dwelling in glory. Do this so that we would have a desire to be dissolved and go to him who died for us and so that whether we wake up or pass away, we should live together with him.

We ask you to bless people everywhere, famous or unknown, rich or poor, so that they would all faithfully serve you and enjoy whatever you determine they need. We especially ask that you would arrange stability and peace in the affairs of this world through your providence. We ask this so that your church can joyfully serve you in all quietness.

We leave all we have with you, especially our friends and those who are dear to us. We desire that when we are dead and gone that they would similarly lift their souls to you. Teach those who come after us to praise, love, and obey you. And if we wake in the morning, may we praise you again with joyful lips, still offering ourselves to you as a more acceptable sacrifice through Jesus in whose words we beg you to hear us.

95. Prayer for Right Perspective
William Jay (1769–1853) ❧ *39*

Oh Lord, help us remember that gratitude is more fitting to us than complaint. Our afflictions, indeed, have been light compared to our guilt. They have been few compared to the sufferings of others. They have all been attended with innumerable alleviations. They have all been necessary, all given to us with a regard for our welfare, all designed to work together for our good. We bless you for what is past, and we trust you for what is to come. Indeed, we cast all our cares upon you, knowing that you care for us.

96. Prayer for God's Guidance
William Jay (1769–1853) ❧ *39*

God of all grace, Father of mercies, hope of Israel, Savior in time of trouble, why have you revealed yourself in such lovely characters and endearing relations if not to meet our despair, to remove our fears, and to induce us to say, "It is good for me to draw near to God" [Ps. 73:28]?

We come to you as criminals to be pardoned, as beggars to obtain relief, and as friends to enjoy communion with the God of love. We bow down in submission and gratitude to the method that you have appointed and made known for all interactions between you and us. We approach you through Jesus, in whom you have proclaimed yourself to be well pleased, pleading the propitiation of his blood and making mention of his righteousness—and his alone.

What we do not know, teach us. Lead us into all truth. May we see divine things in a divine light so that while they inform our judgment, they may sanctify our heart and consecrate our whole life to the service and glory of God.

Who can understand his own errors? Cleanse us from our secret faults. Search us, oh God, and know our hearts; try us and know our thoughts; and see if there is any wicked way in us. Lead us in the way everlasting.

Accept our collected thanks for the preservation and refreshment of the past night. Take us under your guiding and guardianship this day. Whether we eat or drink or whatever we do, let it all be to the glory of God, through our Lord and Savior. Amen.

97. Prayer for Growing Faith
William Jay (1769–1853) ❧ *39*

You are the author of all existence and the source of all blessedness. We adore you for making us capable of knowing you, for giving us reason and conscience, and for leading us to inquire about you as our Maker who gives songs in the night. We praise you for the wealth of information that you have given us to bring us to you, especially the revelation of the gospel. Here we look into your very heart and see that it is the dwelling place of pity. Here we see your thoughts toward us and find that they are thoughts of peace and not of evil. Here we see you waiting to be gracious and exalted to have mercy. Here you have told our consciences how the guilty can be pardoned, the unholy can be sanctified, and the poor furnished with unsearchable riches.

May we be found in the number of those who do not only hear but who actually know the joyful sound so that we may walk in the light of your countenance, rejoice in your name all day, and be exalted in your righteousness. May we take you, the God of truth, at your word and believe the record that you have given us eternal life and that this life is in your Son. Since it is not only a faithful saying but one that is worthy of all acceptance that he came into the world to save sinners, to him alone we look for salvation, and we do so with all the earnestness the infinite importance of the case requires.

98. Prayer for God's Presence and Closeness
Charles Spurgeon (1834–1892) ❧ *40*

Oh you, who are King of kings and Lord of lords, we worship you.

> Before Jehovah's awe-inspiring throne,
> We bow with sacred joy.[1]

We can truly say that we delight in God. There was a time when we feared you, God, as if you would bind and destroy us. Now we revere you, but we love you as much as we revere. The thought of your omnipresence once terrified us. We said, "Where shall I flee from your presence? [Ps. 139:7]," and saying so made hell itself seem even more dreadful, because we heard a voice, "If I make my bed in hell, you are there! [Ps. 139:8]."

But now, oh Lord, we desire to find you. Our longing is to feel your presence, and your presence is the heaven of heavens. When you are there, a sick bed is soft. When you are there, the furnace of affliction grows cool. When you are there, the

---

1 Isaac Watts, "Before Jehovah's Awful Throne" (1705).

house of prayer is none other than the house of God—it is the very gate of heaven!

So come near, our Father; come very near to your children. Some of us are very weak in body and faint in heart. Without delay, oh God, lay your powerful hand on us and say to us, "Fear not." Perhaps some of us like the world too much, which makes the world attractive to us. Come near to kill the influence of the world with your superior power.

Even worship may not seem easy to some. The Dragon seems to pursue them, and floods from his mouth wash away their devotion. Give them great eagle's wings so that they can fly away to the place you prepared for them, and cause them to rest in the presence of God today.

Our Father, come and give rest to your children now. Take the helmet from our brow. Relieve the heavy weight of our armor for a moment. May we just have peace, perfect peace, and be at rest.

Oh, help us, we ask you now! Just as you have already washed your people in the fountain filled with blood and they are clean, now wash us this morning from all defilement in that same water. With the basin and pitcher, Master, wash our feet again. It will greatly refresh us. It will prepare us for the intimate fellowship with you. The priests did the same each time they went into the holy place.

Lord Jesus, take away everything that would hinder the closest communion with God. We ask you to remove any wish or desire that might hamper us in prayer. Take away right now any memory of either sorrow or care that keeps us from fixing our affection wholly on our God. What do we have to do with idols anymore? You have seen and observed us. You know where the difficulties lie. Help us against idolatry, and may we come boldly, not merely into some holy place, but into the holiest place of all, your presence, where we would never dare to come if our great Lord had not torn the veil, sprinkled the mercy seat with his own blood, and summoned us to enter.

Now we have come close to you—to the light that shines between the wings of cherubim—and we speak to you now as a man speaks to his friends. Our God, we are yours. You are ours. We are about one thing; we are allies together for one battle. Your battle is our battle, and our fight is yours. We ask you to help us. You who made archangel Michael and his angels strong enough to cast out the Dragon and his demons, help our weak flesh and blood so that your word would be fulfilled in us—"The God of peace will soon crush Satan under your feet [Rom. 16:20]."

Our Father, we are very weak. Worst of all, we are very wicked if left to ourselves, and we quickly fall prey to the enemy. So help us! We confess that sometimes in prayer—at the very moments when we are closest to you—some evil thought, some wicked desire comes to mind. Oh, what poor fools we are! Lord, help us. Now we want to come even closer to you and hide under the shadow of your wings. We wish to be lost in you. We pray that you would live in us, and that it would not be we who live but Christ who lives in us, showing himself in us and through us.

Lord, sanctify us. Oh, that your Spirit would come and saturate every ability, subdue every passion, and use every power of our nature for obedience to God.

Come, Holy Spirit; we do know you. You have often overshadowed us. Come, take more possession of us. We feel as if we are standing right at the mercy seat and now our greatest prayer is for perfect holiness, complete consecration, entire cleansing from every evil. Take our heart, our head, our hands, our feet, and use all of it for yourself.

Lord, take our wealth. Let us not hoard it for ourselves, nor spend it on ourselves. Take our talent. Let us not try to educate ourselves so that we have the reputation of intelligence. Instead, let every intellectual pursuit allow us to serve you better.

May every breath be for you. May every minute be spent for you. Help us to live while we live. While we are busy in the world—as we must be because you called us to it—may we sanctify the world for your service. May we be lumps of salt in society. May our spirit and temper, as well as our conversation, be heavenly. May there be an influence about us that would make the world better before we leave it. Lord, hear us in this thing.

And now that we have your ear, we want to pray for the poor world in which we live. We are often horrified by it. Oh Lord, we could wish that we knew nothing of it for our own comfort. Instead, we have said, "Oh, for a lodge in some vast wilderness!"[2] We hear of oppression and robbery and murder, and men seem let loose against each other. Lord, have mercy on this great and wicked city. What is to be done with these millions of people? What can we do? Help every one of your children to do the most each can. May none of us contribute to evil directly or indirectly, but may we contribute to the good of our city.

We now feel that we may speak with you about this because when your servant Abraham stood before you and spoke with such wonderful familiarity to you, he pleaded for Sodom. We now plead for our city. We will follow the example of the

2 William Cowper, "The Timepiece," line 1 in *Poems, of the Inner Temple, Esq. Volume the second. Containing The Task, An Epistle to Joseph Hill, Esq. Tirocinium, or a Review of Schools, And The History of John Gilpin. Fit suculus arbor. Anonym* (London: Printed for J. Johnson, 1786).

father of the faithful and pray for all great cities and, indeed, for all nations. Lord, let your kingdom come. Send forth your light and truth. Chase the old Dragon from his throne, with all his hellish crew. Oh, that the day might come when even on the earth the Son of the woman, the Man-child, should rule the nations—not with a broken staff of wood but with an enduring scepter of iron, full of mercy but full of power, full of grace yet irresistible. Oh, that his rule might soon come, the personal advent of our Lord! We long for the millennial triumph of his word.

Until then Lord, gird us for the fight, and make us to be among those who overcome through the blood of the Lamb and through the word of our testimony because we "loved not our lives even unto death" [Rev. 12:11].

We also lift our voice to you in prayer for all of our dear ones. Lord, bless the sick and make them well as soon as it is right they should be. Sanctify them through what they are enduring until the work is complete. Some of our dear friends are very weak, and some are in deep dread. God, bless them while they suffer in this mortal life that your word compares to a tent. May they look inside with calm joy because we will, in some future time, "put on our heavenly dwelling" [2 Cor. 5:2]. Lord, help us to not be attached too strongly to these things on earth. Let us live here like strangers and treat this world not like our home but like an inn where we stay for a night, knowing we will be on our way tomorrow.

Lord, save the unconverted, and we ask you to bring out those from the converted who have not yet confessed Christ through baptism. May the church be built up by many who are baptized upon their faith in the Father, Son, and Holy Spirit. We pray you would go on and multiply your followers in this nation. Oh, that you would turn people's hearts to the gospel once more. I, your servant, often have a heavy heart because people leave the faith. Bring them back. Do not let Satan take away any more of the stars with his tail, but may the lamps of God shine bright. You, the one who walks among the seven gold lampstands, trim the wick and refill the lamp oil. Let the gospel light shine brightly and steadily.

Now, Lord, we cannot pray any longer, though we have a thousand things to ask for. I, your servant, cannot, so I ask you to leave this unfinished prayer at the mercy seat with this last word: we ask these things in the name of Jesus Christ, your Son. Amen.

99. Prayer for the Church and Society
Charles Spurgeon (1834–1892) ❧ *40*

Oh God, we would not speak to you from a distance nor stand at a distance from the burning mountain like trembling

Israel. No, we have not come to Mount Sinai but to Mount Zion. That is a place for holy joy and thankfulness, not for terror and bondage. We bless your name, oh Lord! We have learned to call you "our Father who is in heaven" [Matt. 6:9]. We do have reverence, for you are in heaven, but we have sweet familiarity, for you are our Father.

Now, we will draw very near to you through Jesus Christ the mediator, and we will boldly speak to you as a man speaks to with his friends because was it not you who said by your Spirit, "Let us then with confidence draw near to the throne of grace" [Heb. 4:16]? We would probably run from your face if we had only remembered our sinfulness. Lord, we do remember it with shame and sorrow, and we are grieved to think we could have offended you or neglected your sweet love and tender mercy for too long. However, we returned to the "Shepherd and Overseer of our souls" [1 Pet. 2:25]. Led by such grace, we look to him whom we crucified, and we have mourned for him and then mourned for our sin.

Now Lord, we confess our guilt before you with tenderness of heart. We pray you would reinforce in the heart of every believer that full and free and perfect and irreversible promise of forgiveness that you gave to all who put their trust in Jesus Christ. Lord, you said it: "If we confess our sins, You are faithful and just to forgive us our sins and to cleanse us from all unrighteousness" [1 John 1:9]. You heard our sin confessed. You receive Christ as the ransom accepted, so we now know we have peace with you. And we bless that glorious one who has come to "finish the transgression, to put an end to sin" [Dan. 9:24], to bring in everlasting righteousness, which by faith we claim as our own and that you do impute onto us.

Now, Lord, would you please make all your children's hearts to dance for joy? Help your people to come to Jesus again today. May we look at him today as we did at the start. May we never take our eyes off from his divine person, his infinite merit, his finished work, his living power, or the expectation of his speeding coming to "judge the world in righteousness, and the peoples in his faithfulness" [Ps. 96:13].

Bless all your people with some special gift, and if we can choose what it is, make it this: "Give me life, O Lord, according to Your word!" [Ps. 119:107]. We have life. Give us life more abundantly. Oh, that we would have so much life that rivers of living water would flow out of us. The Lord makes us useful. Do then, dear Savior, use the very least among us. Take the one talent, and put it to interest for the great Father. Would you please show each one of us what you would have us do? May we be serving you in our families, our business, and the walks of ordinary life. And may we regularly testify about your name, helping in some way to scatter the light amid the evergrowing darkness. From now on and everywhere we go, may we have been sowing some seed that we will bring with us on our shoulders in the form of sheaves of blessing.

Oh God, bless our efforts to evangelize our neighbors. Give us a greater interest in this work so that there would be plenty of men and women who would gladly teach the young. Impress this need upon your people right now, Lord. Move men who have the gifts and ability to preach the gospel. Many people live in places where there is no gospel preaching near them. Lord, make them preach themselves. Will you move some people with such power that they cannot keep quiet about the gospel? Would you see that any attempts—either personally or supporting one who goes—to succeed in bringing the gospel into spiritually dark neighborhoods so that people may know the truth?

Oh Lord, stir up those who live in this vast city. Arouse us to the spiritual destitution of the masses. Oh God, help us by some means—any means, by every means!—to get at the ears of people for Christ's sake so that we may reach their hearts. We do send up a very loud and impassioned cry to you on behalf of the millions that enter no place of Christian worship but violate its sanctity and despise its blessed message with their absence. Lord, wake up our city, we beg you! Send us another Jonah! Send us another John the Baptist! Oh, that the Christ himself would send multitudes of laborers into this ready harvest, because the harvest truly is plentiful, but there are few laborers. Oh God, save this city. Save this country. Save all countries! Let your kingdom come, and may every knee bow and confess that Jesus Christ is Lord.

Our most earnest prayers go up to heaven to you now for great sinners, for men and women who are polluted and depraved by the filthiest of sins. With sovereign mercy, make a raid among them. Come and capture some of these sinners so that they may become great lovers of the one who will surely forgive them. Make them great champions for the cross.

Now, Lord, look upon the multitudes of rich people in this city who know nothing about the gospel and willfully ignore it. Oh, that somehow the impoverished rich would become truly rich in the gospel of Jesus Christ. Then, Lord, look upon the multitude of the poor and working class who think religion to be an unnecessary thing for them. We pray you would get them to think clearly and bring them to listen to the faith that comes by hearing, and hearing by the word of God by any means.

Above all, Holy Spirit, descend in more power. God, would you flood the land until there are streams of righteousness? Is there not a promise that you "will pour water on the thirsty land, and streams on the dry ground" [Isa. 44:3]? Lord, make your people pray. Stir up the church to greater prayerfulness.

Now, as you have commanded, we pray for the people among whom we live. We pray for those in authority, that you would grant a blessing to all judges and rulers, as well as the poor and lowest of the low. Lord, bless all the people. Let the people praise you, oh God! Yes. Let the people praise you for Jesus Christ's sake. Amen and amen.

100. Prayer for Christ's Return
John the apostle, Revelation 22:20–21

He who testifies to these things says, "Surely I am coming soon." Amen. Come, Lord Jesus! The grace of the Lord Jesus be with all. Amen.

PART 2

HISTORICAL
INTRODUCTIONS

5

Early Church (100–800)

❧ 1. The Didache (ca. 100)

The work known commonly as the Didache has a lengthy history of use in the church, both as a book of order and a practical liturgy. The document actually has two different titles. The short one, from which *Didache* is derived, is *The Teaching of the Twelve Apostles* (Διδαχη των δωδεκα αποστολων), while the longer version, *The Teaching of the Lord through the Twelve Apostles to the Nations* (Διδαχη κυριου δια των δωδεκα αποστολων τοις εθνεσιν), focuses on the teachings of Christ. The modern version of the work includes sixteen chapters, which are normally divided into four sections. The first six chapters serve as a catechetical work for baptismal candidates, covering the basics of the faith for new believers. The second section provides a liturgical structure for the church's worship gatherings, the third discusses the ecclesiastical structure of the local congregation, and the last section gives an eschatologically focused benediction. Most scholars accept the tradition that this work can rightly be attributed to the days of the apostles with the date of composition being no later than the middle of the second century.

The prayer included in our volume ("Holy Father, we thank you for your holy name") comes from the liturgical section of the Didache. Found in the tenth chapter, this prayer would have been originally said after the congregation received the elements of the Lord's Supper and thus focuses on the gratitude rightly due to the Father for the gifts he has given "through Jesus, [his] servant." The bread and the cup of the Eucharist serve as tangible reminders of those gifts, but they are certainly not the totality of the gifts, so those who are praying ask God to remember his people, and, with an eschatological turn, they note the temporary nature of the physical world and long for Christ's return.

Source

3: Roswell D. Hitchcock and Francis Brown, eds. *The Teaching of the Twelve Apostles: Edited with a Translation, Introduction and Notes* (London: John C. Nimmo, 1885), 18–21.

✎ 2. Clement of Rome (d. ca. 99)

According to several early church sources, Clement served as a bishop of the church at Rome at the end of the first century. Though the specific details of this position have been debated, virtually all modern scholars accept Clement as a leader of the Roman church whose ministry also included a close connection to the church at Corinth. That congregation, the recipient of two canonical epistles from Paul, evidently experienced continuing struggles regarding its leadership and thus received the correspondence from Clement now known as *1 Clement*. Though little is known about his early life, Clement was associated with the apostle Peter during their time in Rome—according to Tertullian, Peter ordained Clement as his successor in Rome. At the end of his ministry, Clement was imprisoned by Trajan. Yet, he continued his ministry there, focusing mainly on fellow prisoners, until he eventually suffered martyrdom by being tied to an anchor and tossed into the sea.

The prayer included in our volume ("Grant us, Lord God, a hope in the fount of all creation") is taken from *1 Clement*. The passage demonstrates Clement's pastoral care both for his own congregations in Rome as well as for the troubled church in Corinth and, indeed, for the global church as a whole. Overall, the constant refrain from this persecuted pastor focuses on the consistency of the God he serves—the God who loves him and his people and sovereignly rules over every aspect of his creation.

Sources

4: Joseph Barber Lightfoot, ed. *The Apostolic Fathers* (London: MacMillan, 1890), 2:172–81; Kirsopp Lake, ed. *The Apostolic Fathers* (New York: MacMillan, 1912), 1:110–16.

3. Polycarp (69–155)

Polycarp served as bishop of Smyrna, having been discipled by the apostle John. Polycarp has long been honored—alongside Clement of Rome and Ignatius of Antioch—as one of the three most prominent apostolic fathers. A single work attributed to his hand, *The Epistle of Polycarp to the Philippians*, remains extant. That work, along with the account of his death entitled *The Martyrdom of Polycarp*, provides modern readers with access to his story. Little is known of his life, but according to Irenaeus (one of Polycarp's disciples and a well-known leader of the church in the next generation), Polycarp had been in contact with several people who had seen the risen Christ.

Two major events came about because of his role as bishop in Smyrna. First, Polycarp traveled to Rome to meet with church leaders there regarding the celebration of Easter. Those meetings proved to be unsuccessful at determining an agreed upon date, and Polycarp aimed to return to Smyrna. However, he was arrested by the Roman proconsul and ultimately martyred for his faith, an event that is recorded in *The Martyrdom of Polycarp*.

Polycarp's ecclesiastical position in Smyrna also made him a sought-after counselor and led him to pen an official letter to the Philippian church, which contains the prayer included in our volume ("May God, the Father of our Lord Jesus Christ, the eternal high priest"). The letter itself serves as an early witness to the presence of New Testament works, quoting from Matthew, Luke, Acts, and the letters from Peter and John. Though the prayer contained here has been conserved for posterity by ancient Latin texts rather than the original Greek text, scholars do not doubt its authenticity. Overall, the prayer reflects Polycarp's godly desires for this congregation to be fortified by God and to display the righteous fruits of holy living that comes only from a close relationship with him.

Further, Polycarp's "Oh Lord God Almighty, Father of your beloved and blessed Son" provides the modern reader with a reported account of his last words as he faced death at the hands of the Roman government. The prayer (and the rest of the record of his martyrdom) has a lengthy attestation in the life of the church, though its earliest provenance remains a mystery. Whether this is exactly what Polycarp said at his execution cannot be known, but the content has been received from the earliest days as matching the character of Polycarp. The early church, indeed, saw martyrdom as an honor bestowed by God on the disciple, and this intimate prayer echoes those sentiments.

Sources

5: Kirsopp Lake, ed. *The Apostolic Fathers* (New York: MacMillan, 1912), 1:298.

6: Alexander Roberts, James Donaldson, and A. Cleveland Coxe, eds., "The Encyclical Epistle of the Church at Smyrna," in *The Apostolic Fathers with Justin Martyr and Irenaeus*, vol. 1, *The Ante-Nicene Fathers* (Buffalo, NY: Christian Literature, 1885), 42.

❧ 4. Hippolytus of Rome (ca. 170–ca. 235)

Hippolytus has been associated with a wide variety of Christian communities during the early days of the third century. Scholars as early as Jerome and Eusebius, writing approximately a hundred years after Hippolytus's death, noted the mystery surrounding this community. Theories abound—including a falling out between Hippolytus and the leaders of the church at Rome—but none have been proven. If an issue existed between Hippolytus and the church, it almost certainly was rectified before his martyrdom. According to tradition, Hippolytus was exiled to the mines at Sardinia where he died in 235.

Hippolytus wrote broadly and extensively, providing the church with a variety of biblical commentaries, polemical apologies, and pastoral liturgies. As with most early church leaders, some works attributed to Hippolytus may not have been written by his hand. The undisputed works alone make Hippolytus a leading figure in his day as well as a significant theologian for understanding the history of doctrine.

The prayer included in our volume ("We ask that you send the Holy Spirit") comes from the *Apostolic Tradition*, an anonymous work that has been attributed to Hippolytus since his authorship was first suggested by Eduard von der Goltz in 1906. Most scholars have accepted this attribution though others see this work as a compilation developed over time, finding its final form at some point in the fourth century. Regardless, the prayer—known as "The Anaphora"—fits the ministry and theology of Hippolytus. In it, he asks the triune God to care for his people so that the church might be strengthened in their faith. This prayer would have been used in the liturgy of the church, after the celebration of the Eucharist, and would have probably ended the service.

Source

7: Edmund Hauler, *Didascaliae Apostolorum Fragmenta ueronensia Latina* (Teubneri, 1900), 107.

5. The Clementine Liturgy (ca. mid-third century)

The so-called Clementine Liturgy gets its name from being attributed to Clement of Rome in a late Greek collection of liturgical writings. Other published versions use the title *Liturgy of Saint James*. Regardless, scholars have generally accepted the ancient nature of this text, which has long been connected to the church in Jerusalem, with its influence spreading beyond that singular congregation. In the nineteenth century, the British liturgical scholar Charles Edward Hammond (1837–1914) noted the similarities between this liturgy and the one described by Justin Martyr (also associated with the congregations meeting in Rome in the second century). This notable similarity may well be the reason for the later connection with Clement.

The Greek texts of these prayers are readily available both in seventeenth-century reproductions and in later publications, including those collected by Hammond. On the whole, the two texts largely agree with one another. Where disagreements occur, the translator has made decisions to aid in the usefulness and readability to the current audience.

The first prayer ("Oh great and mighty God, unequaled in counsel") included in our volume was originally meant to be said before the dispersal of the Lord's Supper. The prayer is one of introspection and confession, intended to help the congregation refocus their minds on the magnitude of the divine glory and the otherness of God.

The second prayer ("We pray for those who hate us") is a heartfelt prayer for those who would persecute the church or who have otherwise removed themselves from the congregation. The penitent prays for God's mercy on those who find themselves—for one reason or another—outside the church.

Finally, the third prayer ("Oh Lord God Almighty, who hears the prayers of the upright") acknowledges believers' dependence on God, seeks his protection for those within and over the church, and provides language for people in all stations of life—marrieds, singles, children, and parents.

Sources

8, 9, 11: C. F. Hammond, ed. *Liturgies Eastern and Western* (Oxford: MacMillan, 1878), 3–24.

10: *The Ancient Liturgy of the Church of Jerusalem* (London, 1744), 93–97.

❧ 6. Syrian Clementine Liturgy

The prayer from the Syrian Clementine Liturgy ("Oh God, the unfathomable abyss of peace") comes to the modern reader with a long history of communal use. Like our other texts from ancient liturgies, its attribution (to Clement) is more of a statement of association than a statement of original authorship. This prayer can be traced to the earliest days of the church that spoke Aramaic (which a small but significant population of Christians continue to speak, even in the twenty-first century) and can be found in Greek texts that provide various orders of worship for the ancient church. This beautiful congregational prayer focuses on the desire for peace in this church, which quickly experienced division between various language groups as well as theological developments. Overall, it points the congregation to the magnitude of God's greatness as the only firm foundation for spiritual maturity and authentic community.

Source

11: William Bright, *Ancient Collects and Other Prayers, Selected for Devotional Use from Various Rituals* (Oxford: J.H. and Jas. Parker, 1862), 80.

❧ 7. Liturgy of Saint Chrysostom

The worship manual known as the *Liturgy of Saint Chryso-stom*, like the other ancient liturgies, has a lengthy history of use in ancient traditions. As the name suggests, it has an early connection with John Chrysostom, who served in ecclesiastical leadership in Antioch before being appointed archbishop of Constantinople in 397. This liturgy probably developed in the church in Antioch before being formalized in Constantinople. As such, the content of the prayers may have originated quite a while before Chrysostom's ministry.

The prayer that begins "Almighty God, who has given us the grace necessary" is a corporate prayer that acknowledges and engenders total reliance on God. It includes a request for God to answer but also an acknowledgement of the limitations of human understanding and a recognition of God's omnibenevolence regardless of how he answers. Though the prayer itself does not appear in the earliest manuscripts of this liturgy, it does appear in later (yet still ancient) liturgies of the ancient church. The text for this prayer is a modernized version of the sixteenth-century text included in the Book of Common Prayer. Overall, this prayer appears in numerous liturgies throughout Christendom.

"Dear Lord, remember this city" turns the attention of the praying congregation to the global church, moving the focus beyond the gathered body to all of those who are called by God's name. In sum, this prayer encourages the church to remember those who face numerous dangers—whether from traveling, sickness, or enslavement—and poetically asks for God's gracious eye on those who "cultivate the soil" of the church.

Sources

12: *The booke of common prayer* [. . .] (1549), xxiiii.

13: John Mason Neale, *The Liturgies of S. Mark, S. James, S. Clement, S. Chrysostom, and the Church of Malabar* (London: AMS, 1859), 139–40.

❧ 8. Old Gallican Rite

The *Old Gallican Rite* is a collection of liturgical works from the ancient church of what is now modern-day France. The first records of this church date to the early second century and are connected to the ministry of Irenaeus (ca. 130–ca. 202), bishop of Lyon, who recorded the deaths of the martyrs of that city in 177. From an early date, then, this community of believers suffered great persecution and developed a notable congregational worship pattern, complete with numerous prayers that continue to speak to believers today. We have given the prayers that were originally in Latin or earlier English a new English translation.

The prayer entitled "Grant holiness to new believers" allows the entire gathered congregation to pray for the new catechumens in their midst. However, this prayer can also apply to mature believers.

"May Jesus, our God, the first and the last, living unto the ages of ages" is a poignant prayer intended to precede the public reading of Scripture. This prayer focuses both on the church member who is preparing to read Scripture in a congregational service and on those who will be listening. The very fact that the early church had a written prayer for this occasion speaks loudly to their view of the importance of the public reading of Scripture.

The early church also turned its attention to the unity of the church as a whole in the prayer entitled "Lord Jesus Christ, you said to your apostles." Remembering Jesus's provision of peace for his apostles served as a reminder of his high priestly prayer for unity. This prayer asks for the church today to be gathered into that divine unity.

Recognizing the continuing work of God in both delivering and protecting his people from sin, the prayer entitled "Being delivered from evil" asks God not only to continue in that divine work but also to provide additional protection from emboldened enemies. In both battles—against external enemies and internal ones—believers need God to act on their behalf. This text sometimes appears in the Mozarabic liturgy, another closely related family of liturgical texts, rather than the Gallican family.

Early Christian prayers that mention the dead, such as the one here, are seeking to express thankfulness for a particular person's life. Such prayers do not reflect what would later become the medieval theological perspectives on purgatory and death but rather demonstrate a conviction that believers who died in grace were with Christ.[1]

The prayer that begins "It is right and just, indeed it is fair and just, for us to praise you" notes the presence of the Trinity in the people of God. This particular prayer reminds the church of the divine seal on their lives through the presence of the Holy Spirit.

The prayer "It is right and just for us to give thanks to you" is a prayer of thanksgiving steeped in redemptive theology. It focuses the penitent on how God uses even the most horrific of wrongs—the original sin of Adam—to bring about his

---

1   For information on how the early church could have understood prayers for the dead, see James B. Gould, *Understanding Prayer for the Dead: Its Foundation in History and Logic* (Eugene, OR: Cascade Books, 2016), 21–25.

good and righteous plan. The salvific work of the new Adam is juxtaposed against the failure of the old Adam, and the church is given the opportunity to rejoice.

In "It is truly right and just to pray with enthusiasm," the church asks the triune God to care for it so that it can grow in safety and with the protection of divine acceptance. Last, in a touching reminder of the bonds of friendship, the prayer "Have mercy, oh Lord, on all those whom you have associated with us" turns the congregation to an important task of the community—for all to be working toward godliness and conformity to the Lord's holy will.

The Old Gallican Rite, like most liturgical works, also provides prayers for daily life. "Abba, Father, fulfill the office of your name" was a prayer intended for mealtimes but appropriate for other activities as well. It leads believers to remind themselves that they need to be filled with love for God.

Sources

14: Selina Fitzherbert Fox, ed., *A Chain of Prayer Across the Ages* (London: John Murray, 1915), 135.

15: "The Divine Liturgy of St Germanus of Paris" Eglise Catholique Orthodoxe de France, April 22, 2019, https://eglise-catholique -orthodoxe-de-france.fr/.

16–17: C. F. Hammond, ed. *Liturgies Eastern and Western* (Oxford: MacMillan, 1878), 345–48.

18–20: John Mason Neale, *The Liturgies of S. Mark, S. James, S. Clement, S. Chrysostom, and the Church of Malabar* (London: AMS, 1859), 106–7.

21: Selina Fitzherbert Fox, ed., *A Chain of Prayer Across the Ages* (London: John Murray, 1915), 20.

22: Manning Potts, *Prayers of the Early Church* (Nashville: Upper Room, 1953), 38.

9. Liturgy of Jerusalem and Saint James

The liturgy traditionally believed to be used by the church of Jerusalem has also been associated with James, the brother of Jesus, who became a leader there (Acts 15). It is an order of congregational worship that has probably been in use since the first century, although the form that has been preserved into modernity probably dates from the fourth century. The full liturgy is lengthy (several hours if completed as written) and is still used in Eastern churches, specifically on days honoring James.

The three prayers included in our volume demonstrate different aspects of the liturgy. First, "Help us, oh Lord, lover of humanity" (here translated from the Greek text) offers a congregational cry for God's aid in everyday living and communal worship. Second, "Oh Lord, Jesus Christ, the Son of the living God" reiterates the need for God to act in the life of believers, recognizing the constant struggles common to humanity and declaring our inability to overcome those struggles apart from divine intervention. Last, "Oh good God, by the grace of Christ" notes believers' incessant fight against their sin nature and requests God's help to remove sins that continue to cause trouble.

Source

23–25: *The ancient liturgy of the Church of Jerusalem, being the liturgy of St. James* [. . .] (London, 1744), 72, 107.

10. Liturgy of Saint Mark

The Liturgy of Saint Mark is the liturgical manual used by the Orthodox church of Alexandria. It is the oldest attested liturgy in the Orthodox Church, having a documentary witness dating to the late fourth century. The liturgy is still used in the Orthodox Church on the feast day for Mark the Evangelist. The prayers included in our volume are modernized versions of older English translations used in various regions in the Orthodox Church.

The first prayer from the liturgy, "We beg of you, oh lover of humanity," reminds the church to continue walking in faith and begs God for the perseverance that only comes from him. The beautiful (albeit common) theme of God as a haven for the shipwrecked appears in this liturgical prayer as the Christian requests God's assistance for all believers who are facing turmoil.

The next prayer included in our volume, "Oh God of light," asks the Lord for enlightenment and understanding as he provides unique gifts of divine pleasure. Finally, "We give you thanks—more than thanks" allows the penitent to express gratitude for arriving at the very moment of the prayer, recognizing that even the faithful cannot demand anything of God. In this prayer, the congregation notes their desire and hope for God to protect them from all temptations and to enable each believer to live a life free from sin.

Sources

26: Selina Fitzherbert Fox, ed., *A Chain of Prayer Across the Ages* (London: John Murray, 1915), 41.

27–28: James Donaldson, trans., *The Ante-Nicene Fathers*, vol. 7, edited by Alexander Roberts, James Donaldson, and A. Cleveland Coxe (Buffalo, NY: Christian Literature, 1886), 551, 558.

✤ 11. Coptic Liturgy of Saint Cyril

Cyril (ca. 376–444) served as the patriarch of Alexandria at a time when the city held great significance in the Roman Empire. His stance against the teachings of Nestorius, patriarch of Constantinople, and (especially) John of Antioch came to a head at the Council of Ephesus in 431. His theological stances made his legacy a lasting one that reached even into the worship services of the church. Whether he actually wrote the liturgy that bears his name is not known, but tradition attaches it to the time of his leadership.

In the touching prayer "Oh God of love who has given a new commandment"—taken from the liturgy of the Coptic church, a church in the Alexandrian tradition associated with Cyril of Alexandria—the congregation begs God to remove memories of difficult events from the past, especially those caused by the ill will of others.

Sources

29: Manning Potts, *Prayers of the Early Church* (Nashville: Upper Room, 1953), 42.

The booke of common prayer [. . .] (London: James Bettenham, 1549)

John Mason Neale, *The Liturgies of S. Mark, S. James, S. Clement, S. Chrysostom, and the Church of Malabar* (London: AMS, 1859).

John Mason Neale and G. H. Forbes, *The Ancient Liturgies of the Gallican Church* (Burntisland: AMS, 1855).

❧ 12. Cyprian (ca. 210–258)

As a member of a wealthy family in the metropolis of Carthage at the beginning of the third century, Cyprian received an excellent education and began his adult life as an orator and rhetorician. He converted to Christianity and was baptized in adulthood (when he was about thirty-five years old) and quickly moved into the diaconate and, ultimately, the bishopric of Carthage. From that position, Cyprian shepherded the church in North Africa during the Decian persecution and the accompanying controversies regarding the reconciliation of the lapsed (those who fell away from the faith in the midst of persecution) with the faithful. The so-called Novatian controversy (during which time Cyprian's opponents elected rival bishops in both Carthage and Rome) pressed the church toward significant reconsiderations of both the roles of the lapsed as well as the influence of individual pastorates and councils of ecclesiastical leaders.

When persecution again erupted in Carthage under Emperor Valerian, Cyprian refused to conform to the government's requirements. He was successively banished, then imprisoned, and finally executed for his faith. He died by the sword—after being publicly examined by the Roman authorities—on September 14, 258.

Cyprian's written legacy can be found in his constant pastoral care both for the congregations under his care and for those more remotely associated with his ministry. These extant writings provide helpful insight into his understanding of his role as a prominent church leader during difficult days. The two prayers that are included in this collection ("Christ imparts this saving gracious pardon" and "Let us rouse ourselves as much as we are able") stem from two different writings— a pastoral letter to Demetrian (who opposed Christianity) and an ecclesial call to unity given to the universal church. Both are the closing prayers for their respective works.

Source

30–31: E. B. Pusey, *Library of Fathers of the Holy Catholic Church*, vol. 3 (Oxford: J. H. Parker, 1839), 149, 215.

☙ 13. Hilary of Poitiers (ca. 310–ca. 367)

Hilary became bishop of Poitiers (a city in the western part of modern France) sometime around 350. As a child, he received an excellent education that included studies in Greek classics. At some point in his adult life, he renounced his pagan roots for Christianity and, along with his wife and daughter, was baptized. Later, as bishop, he became embroiled in the Arian controversy and famously corresponded with Emperor

Constantius II on the subject. From 356, Hilary spent about four years in exile because of his doctrinal beliefs, but that exile gave him time to focus on his theological writings, including Latin works wherein he sought to clarify the complexities of Trinitarian theology that had previously only been expounded in Greek.

The prayer included in our volume can be found in a collection of Hilary's writings that has come to be known as *De Trinitate* (*On the Trinity*). In these writings, Hilary dove headfirst into the major theological issue of the day—the nature of the Trinity—and attempted to bring the Greek language behind Nicene orthodoxy to bear on the Latin-speaking world of the West. The lengthy prayer included in our volume ("I know, oh Lord God Almighty, that as the chief duty of my life") recognizes the difficulties of comprehending the transcendent God, especially the mystery of the Trinity. Hilary's concluding request for "precision of language, soundness of argument, grace of style, and loyalty to truth" applies to all who take up the mantle of ecclesial leadership.

Source

32: Philip Schaff and Henry Wace, eds, *A Select Library of the Nicene and Post-Nicene Fathers of the Christian Church: Second Series* (Oxford: Parker, 1898), 9a:50–51.

14. Ephrem the Syrian (ca. 306–373)

As a leading theologian on the eastern side of the Roman Empire, Ephrem was involved in establishing an early version of the university in his hometown of Nisibi. During his time teaching at Nisibi, the town was besieged by the Persians in the aftermath of Constantine's death, and several of the faculty, including Ephrem, moved to Edessa where they continued their pedagogical endeavors. While in Edessa, the school came under fire for their theological beliefs, but Ephrem developed a reputation as an orthodox theologian and a popular hymn-writer. As a member of an early monastic community, Ephrem's ministry in Edessa focused on the school and the local congregation. He ultimately died from complications related to an outbreak of the plague, which he evidently caught while caring for other patients. Ephrem died in June 373.

Ephrem was a voluminous hymn writer; more than four hundred of his songs are still extant. Almost all of those works were originally penned in his native language, a dialect of Aramaic. His moniker "the Syrian" probably stems from the confusion of Aramaic with Syriac in scholarship of the early Middle Ages. Almost all of Ephrem's extant hymns had theological motivations, with one particular collection, *The Hymns Against Heresies*, providing helpful insight into his aims. Evidently, several heretical teachers used hymns as teaching tools, and Ephrem decided this method could also be used to promote orthodoxy. Additionally, Ephrem wrote several commentaries and collections of homilies, which spawned an entire collection of works often attributed to him but clearly produced after his lifetime.

The prayer "Glory to you who clothed yourself in Adam's mortal body" comes from a collection of homilies. It centers on the ultimate condescension of the divine: the incarnation of Jesus Christ. Included in the prayer is a beautiful meditation on the forgiveness offered to those directly involved in his crucifixion—both the event of his death (the sinful act of the perpetrators) and that of his resurrection (the final act that brought about forgiveness) were made possible because he took on flesh.

The second prayer we have included from Ephrem ("Whatever is allowed, let us sing") comes in the form of a hymn wherein the congregation recognizes humanity's dependence on God both to know truth and to be useful in the communication of that truth. Ephrem's poetic presentation clearly shows how God must control the human tongue if it will in any way be useful for godliness. The version included here is in prose, which highlights the supplication.

Sources

33: Philip Schaff and Henry Wace, eds, *A Select Library of the Nicene and Post-Nicene Fathers of the Christian Church: Second Series* (Oxford: Parker, 1898), 13:308–9.

34: J. B. Morris, ed., *Select Works of S. Ephrem the Syrian* (Oxford: John Henry Parker, 1847), 270.

15. Gregory of Nazianzus (329–390)

Known as Gregory the Theologian, Gregory of Nazianzus is one of the Cappadocian Fathers—alongside Gregory of Nyssa and Basil the Great—who developed the theological language used for the promulgation of Trinitarian orthodoxy. The three church leaders were active in the interim between the Councils of Nicea (325) and Constantinople (381) and worked incessantly to combat the teachings of the Pneumatomachian heresy, which denied the personhood of the Holy Spirit.

Gregory's father (Gregory the Elder) served as bishop of Nazianzus and oversaw the younger Gregory's education, starting at home and culminating in Athens where the younger Gregory befriended Basil of Caesarea. After completing his education, young Gregory was ordained as a presbyter by his father (perhaps against his will) and assisted the church in his hometown while also beginning a more academic ministry focused on writing. In these writings, he sought to defend the church, first from the threats of Emperor Julian and later from internal heretical views.

After spending time in the presbytery at Nazianzus, Gregory served as bishop of the newly formed see of Sasima before ultimately being appointed archbishop of Constantinople by Emperor Theodosius I. Gregory had always preferred the introverted life of a writer but felt compelled to serve in more public roles because of the demands of ecclesiastical or secular authorities. In 378, he tendered his resignation from ecclesiastical service, first from Constantinople and then from Nazianzus, where he had served as bishop. He spent his last years at his family's estate in Arianzum, dying in January 390.

Gregory's voluminous writings were as diverse in content as they were in form. He penned a series of poems—some in honor of his friend Basil the Great and another serving as an autobiography—as well as a host of polemical works, theological treatises, and ecclesiastical epistles. The prayers included in our volume showcase a variety of Gregory's genres. The first ("May the only one who has the power to unite") is a new translation from one of his theological orations originally given in Greek. It focuses the reader on the unity found in the Trinitarian Godhead and how that unity is the source of reconciliation for humanity. The second ("As the sun rises, I lift my hand to you") stems from his hymns and poems. This prayer does not have a readily available Greek text, but it has been attributed to Gregory for centuries. Virtually no scholars question the authorship, and the content—displaying an utter dependence on God for protection from sin—fits well with Gregory's other writings.

Sources

35: Allen W. Chatfield, *Songs and Hymns of Earliest Greek Christian Poets, Bishops and Others* (London: Rivingtons, 1876), 120.

36: Arthur James Mason, ed., *The Five Theological Orations of Gregory of Nazianzus* (Cambridge: Cambridge University Press, 1899), 107.

❧ 16. Gregory of Nyssa (ca. 335–ca. 395), Emmelia of Caesarea (d. 375), and Macrina the Younger (d. 379)

Gregory of Nyssa was born into a godly family. His paternal grandfather was martyred, and his paternal grandmother, Macrina the Elder, was a confessor during the persecutions inflicted by Maximinus II. Gregory originally established a career as a rhetorician before ultimately following in the ecclesiastical path of his family. His brothers included Basil the Great (bishop of Caesarea), Peter (bishop of Sebaste), and Naucratius (a hermit who died young but not before developing a reputation for generously caring for the indigent).

As a bishop, Gregory participated in the First Council of Constantinople (381) and was active alongside Basil and Gregory of Nazianzus in the Trinitarian conflicts that arose between the Councils of Nicea and Constantinople. Gregory would ultimately be remembered (along with Basil and Gregory of Nazianzus) as one of the Cappadocian fathers. He wrote several works that have had lasting impact on the church, including a work on the Trinity, but his most influential work is a hagiography of his sister, Macrina the Younger. The modernized version of the prayers included in our volume (both originally translated in 1916) come from that work, *The Life of Saint Macrina*. Gregory records these two prayers ("To you, oh Lord, I offer my first and last children" and "Oh Lord, you have removed the fear of death from me") as the last words of his mother Emmelia and his sister Macrina respectively. Both women lived exemplary lives, spending the majority of their time—after the death of Emmelia's husband—overseeing and providing for a monastic community of women. Macrina's fiancé died before they could get married and, recognizing this as an act of divine providence, she vowed to remain unmarried and gave her life to her family, the church, and especially the new monastic community. These prayers indicate the intense, lifelong passion of these two women, and they provide encouraging and challenging words for the many who have been touched by their stories in the intervening millennia.

Source

37–38: W. K. Lowther Clarke, *The Life of St. Macrina by St. Gregory of Nyssa*, Early Church Classics (London: SPCK, 1916), 39, 55–57.

❧ 17. Augustine of Hippo (354–430)

Augustine of Hippo was the most celebrated theologian of his era and one of the most influential theologians of all time. Raised by his devout Christian mother, Monica, and his Roman father Patricius, Augustine received an excellent education, first in a small village and later in the metropolis of Carthage. That education prepared him well for his initial foray into vocational life when he became professor of rhetoric at Milan in 384. Having already explored various theological positions, Augustine was prepared to meet the celebrated orator and preacher, Bishop Ambrose of Milan. That relationship proved to be a major turning point in Augustine's life as he not only came to faith under Ambrose's influence but also saw his son, Adeodatus, come to faith as well. The two were baptized together on Easter Sunday, 387.

Augustine returned to his home in northern Africa around 389 and founded a monastic community at his familial estate. He became a priest in 391 and later became bishop of Hippo. Throughout his ministry, Augustine remained focused on the spiritual life of those under his pastoral care even while he wrote voluminously. His work ranged from sermons to theological autobiography (his *Confessions*) and polemical theology (he became involved in the majority of the theological controversies of his day, like the fight with Pelagius). Augustine's writings have been studied since their first printing and have found a readership in every successive generation. In the beginning of the sixteenth century, for instance, the leaders of the Protestant Reformation cited Augustine far more often than any other source (except for the Bible).

Each of our translated prayers from Augustine are from his *Confessions*. In this text, Augustine methodically examines his early life in order to understand the deeper theological questions that plague him and his congregants. "You, oh Lord, are great and worthy of exceeding praise" opens the autobiography by asking God for knowledge of him. This prayer includes the famous line, "Our hearts are restless until they rest in you" and forces the reader to consider the nature of prayer itself by questioning whether faith must come before or after initial requests. Significantly, even as Augustine asks for rest from God, even as he begs for the ability to seek God, he recognizes that the necessary prerequisite of faith is itself a gift from God. This point forms the basis of his entire theological system.

"My God, how could I think that you were silent" provides words for the common experience of many (if not most) believers who find themselves in periods of perceived silence from God. For Augustine, this silence came during his well-known dalliance with his besetting sins of lust and fornication. His godly mother Monica pleaded with him to resist those temptations, but the young Augustine refused to listen. As he writes his *Confessions*, he realizes how God was using his faithful servant Monica to bring Augustine to himself. But that realization only arrives with the benefit of hindsight. Such realization leads to his confessional prayer.

The struggles common to a humanity that longs for happiness but cannot find it apart from God form the basis of the prayer that begins, "Oh Lord, have mercy on me! I do not hide my wounds." As this line suggests, Augustine has already realized his own shortcomings. He has wounds; he is sick. And he needs the only doctor capable of healing him.

With this prayer, Augustine speaks boldly for all humans and especially for those in his spiritual care.

Augustine also included prayers throughout his exegetical work, prayers that arose from the sheer need to respond to the text of Scripture as it coursed through his being. "We turn our hearts to the Lord God" in our volume is a modernized version of a nineteenth-century translation from Augustine's work on the Psalms. The prayer, though, is not specific to the Psalms; rather, it serves as a model for the personal and congregational response to the rightly offered sermon.

The prayer found at the end of book fifteen of Augustine's monumental work on the Trinity (*De Trinitate*) is his prayer for his own written works. Having sought to speak rightly about something as complex as the triune Godhead, Augustine prays for God's forgiveness where he has failed. In our new translation from the Latin text ("When we reach you"), Augustine gives voice to so many Christians who dare to speak or write about our great God, recognizing the sheer audacity of such a task.

Sources

39–41: Pius Knöll, ed., *Sancti Aureli Augustini Confessionum Libri Tredecim. Corpus Scriptorum Ecclesiasticorum Latinorum* (Vindobonae: Tempsky, 1896), 33:1–2, 33–34, 256.

42: Philip Schaff, ed., *A Select Library of the Nicene and Post-Nicene Fathers of the Christian Church* (New York: Christian Literature, 1888), 8:683.

43: Jacques Paul Migne, ed., *Patrologiae Cursus Completus*, Series Latina (Paris: Bibliotheca Cleri Universae, 1865), 42:1098.

18. John Cassian (ca. 360–ca. 435)

John Cassian was a Christian theologian of the late fourth century. He was drawn to the monastic life that began gaining popularity during this time, traveling with a close friend to such communities, first in modern Israel and later in the Egyptian desert. As a monastic interested in theological thought, Cassian became embroiled in various heated discussions of the day, particularly the controversies surrounding the teachings of Origen (ca. 184–ca. 253). That first Origenist controversy enveloped the theological wing of the empire, leading (at least in part) to the temporary ousting of the archbishop of Constantinople, John Chrysostom, and involving most of the major theologians of the day. Cassian himself went to Rome to defend his own views and those of his fellow Origenists. While he was visiting Rome, Cassian accepted an invitation to establish a monastic community in modern France near Marseilles. His influence over the various monastic communities in the western Roman Empire stemmed largely from the fact that Benedict of Nursia (who wrote the famous monastic rules titled *The Rule of Saint Benedict*) followed Cassian's teachings in his own monastic orders. Cassian wrote widely, especially during his time in Marseilles. Latin versions of his works were produced in several collections, including *Conferences*, *The Institutes*, and *On the Incarnation of the Lord.*

Cassian pens the prayer "Laying our hands upon that monstrous head of the deadly serpent" in book seven of his *On the Incarnation of the Lord*, which was written as a defense against Nestorianism. The prayer vividly notes the ongoing fight against the schemes of the devil and even against the internal struggles of the sinful self. It reminds the penitent to rely only on the work of the God-man, Jesus Christ, to overwhelm the evil of the world and to bring holy truth to its full exposure.

Source

44: Philip Schaff and Henry Wace, eds, *A Select Library of the Nicene and Post-Nicene Fathers of the Christian Church: Second Series* (Oxford: Parker, 1894), 11:604.

6

Medieval Church (800–1500)

⪼ 19. Bede (673–735)

Often called the Venerable Bede, this monastic figure spent the vast majority of his life at the famous monastery of Saints Peter and Paul at Monkwearmouth-Jarrow. Bede had been sent to the monastery at an early age, some believe as early as seven years old, and spent the entirety of his life at either Monkwearmouth or Jarrow in the modern-day county of Tyne and Wear in the north of England. Bede was a scholar, a church leader, and a theologian, with his most famous work being *The Ecclesiastical History of the English People*, which has had significant influence since its original production in Latin around 731. That work played no small part in developing a sense of unity among the people of the British Isles and has even been credited for establishing a unified English culture.

Bede's historical works, along with his work on dates and calendars, helped popularize the practice of dating events from the birth of Christ.

Bede was a polymath, composing works on grammar, astronomical calculations, and poetry alongside his well-known historical works. After his death, Bede's disciples honored his work and eventually developed a dedicated following. His remains were moved from his native monasteries to the cathedral in nearby Durham in the early eleventh century. At the end of the nineteenth century, his work was officially honored by the Catholic Church when Pope Leo XIII bestowed on him the title "doctor of the church," making Bede the only recipient of the honor who was native to the British Isles.

The prayers included in our volume ("Oh Lord our God, we believe in you," "Savior of souls, Redeemer of the world," and "Be near to me, my only hope") come from Bede's ecclesiastical works, which were intended for use in corporate settings. They focus both on theological orthodoxy—especially Trinitarianism—and on the personal relationship between a sinner and the Holy God. Collectively, these prayers provide an overview of Bede's understanding of the necessity of solid doctrinal teaching to complement the personal experience of the Christian faith.

Source

45–47: J. A. Giles, ed., *The Complete Works of Venerable Bede: In the Original Latin*, vol. 1, Patres Ecclesia Anglicanae (London: Whittaker, 1843), 241–45.

❧ 20. John of Damascus (ca. 675–749)

Born in the Umayyad Caliphate in the late-seventh century, John of Damascus developed an impressive resume as a leading theologian of the church. His polemical writings and apologies laid a foundation for theological discussions in the Eastern church, though he is also considered a doctor of the church in the West. John's father, Sarjun, served as a bureaucrat in the caliphate, a position John may have also held before his ordination as a priest and monk. Overall, John's early education was extensive, and he developed quite a reputation for academic prowess in numerous fields of study.

Sometime around 706, John joined the monastery at Mar Saba in Jerusalem, where he would spend the remainder of his days. During his time in the monastery, he focused his attention on his academic work, writing a number of books against the various heresies that continued to plague the church and on particular issues facing the Eastern empire. Of particular note are John's works on perichoresis (a theological concept used to describe the interpenetration both of

Christ's human and divine natures and of the persons within the triune Godhead) as well as his discussion of the teachings of Islam in his longer work, *Concerning Heresies.*

The first prayer included in our volume ("Oh Lord, with your gracious and merciful eye") stems from a work entitled *Barlaam and Josephat,* which was produced in the Far East and has historically been attributed to John of Damascus. Modern scholarship tends to dismiss this attribution because it is based solely on an early statement that a monk named John wrote the work. Regardless, the prayer has often been associated with John of Damascus and fits well within the broader context of his writings. Though it almost certainly was not written by him, it is included here as a helpful glimpse of the type of prayers attributed to the Damascene tradition. Notably, the Loeb Classical Library includes this work as the only representative writing of John.

The second prayer has a stronger provenance and comes from a collection of John's hymns. This particular prayer, "With pain earth's joys are mingled," is an English translation of John's Greek text. The translation was completed by Richard Frederick Littledale (1833–1890), a nineteenth-century minister in the Church of England and an academic. In the hymn, sung as a prayer to Jesus, John asks for divine rest in the midst of the fallen world that offers, at best, momentary glimpses of joy.

Sources

48: George Ratcliffe Woodward and Harold Mattingly, eds. *Barlaam and Ioasaph*, Loeb Classical Library (Cambridge, MA: Harvard University Press, 1914), 34:526–27.

49: Bernhard Pick, *Hymns and Poetry of the Eastern Church* (New York: Eaton and Mains, 1908), 129–30.

ᔰ 21. Anselm (1033/4–1109)

Anselm was consecrated as archbishop of Canterbury in 1093, but by this time he had already established himself as an academic leader thanks to his time at Bec Abbey, a monastery in the Normandy region of France. At Bec, Anselm succeeded Lanfranc as archbishop as well as leader of the abbey and master of its monastic school.

As archbishop of Canterbury, Anselm often clashed with English nobility, especially over issues of the crown's power to oversee the affairs of the church. In the midst of that turmoil, Anselm turned his attention to writing what would become his most influential work, a theological consideration of the incarnation titled *Cur Deus homo* (*Why God Became Man*). That work introduced the world to Anselm's understanding of the atonement as a matter of divine honor and quickly became foundational for the study of theology.

Anselm wrote numerous other works that dealt with philosophical-theological concerns and peppered these writings with prayers that have since become standalone prayers for use by lay and monastic communities alike. The prayers used in this volume are new translations made from available Latin versions of his work. The prayer "Oh God, I pray that I may so know you and love you" comes from the philosophical work *Proslogion*, a book-length meditation on the attributes of God in which Anselm developed his famous ontological argument for God's existence. In this discussion, Anselm defined the concept of God as the Being than which none greater can be conceived. The prayer included here focuses on the intertwining of this thought experiment with the impassioned joy of personally knowing the one true God.

"Lord Jesus Christ, my Redeemer" comes from an edited collection of Anselm's works and recognizes the feebleness of the human condition. Anselm understands that even his desire is lacking, and he longs for the day when he will be able to give what God deserves.

Another prayer from *Proslogion* ("I implore you, Lord, for my heart is bitter") reminds the reader of the sinner's ultimate need: God's condescension in the midst of difficult situations.

The experience described by Anselm will be familiar to readers both because of his biblical references (he quotes Job and the Psalms) and because of his reflection on common human experiences as he verbalizes the emotions caused by some of life's most difficult moments.

Anselm turns his attention to the presence of the Holy Spirit in his prayer "Come, oh come, most gracious comforter of afflicted souls." Anselm's understanding of true humility—neither an unwarranted deprecation nor an unjust elevation of the self—can be heard in the midst of this intense yearning. Recognizing his own inherent shortcomings, he begs the Holy Spirit to make him acceptable so that he can be pleasing to the triune God.

Keeping a close eye on his own depravity, Anselm consistently writes prayers that recognize his own sin (both intentional and not) and ask for forgiveness from God. "Oh merciful God, indeed, the very author of mercy" provides a beautiful example of Anselm's utter dependence on God. He readily acknowledges that God's presence in his life is the only thing that allows him to know God at all and to be forgiven of everything in his life that falls short of true godliness.

"Hear me, oh Lord, oh great and good Lord" gives words to the heartfelt desire for God to hear one's prayer. Anselm understands that his very desires may be sinful or misled.

Thus, he prays that God would not merely act according to his requests but rather move in his supreme wisdom. By saying this, Anselm reminds himself, those under his spiritual care, and his readership several centuries later that even the reason behind a person's desire to hear from God can be flawed. God alone has the knowledge and wisdom to provide for his people.

Though this prayer mentions the dead, it was not influenced by the doctrine of purgatory that was developed at a later time in the Roman Church but is rather a request for God's grace, pardon, and forgiveness for someone who was waiting for grace. Prior to the Reformation, it was common for liturgies to include prayers for the dead. Such prayers reflected two theological commitments of the medieval church. First, medieval Western Christians were confident that God was a God of the living. Therefore, any Christians who had physically died were not spiritually dead but alive and waiting for their bodily resurrection. Second, medieval Western Christians were not convinced that everyone who died merited entrance into heaven. Therefore, prayers for the dead were supplications for the purification of any sins that would prohibit a person's entrance into the presence of Christ.[1]

---

1   For more information on how the medieval church may have understood prayers for the dead, see James B. Gould, *Understanding Prayer for the Dead: Its Foundation in History and Logic* (Eugene, OR: Cascade Books, 2016), 29–33.

In "I know, oh Lord God, ruler of my life" (often referred to as "A Sinner's Prayer"), Anselm expresses the reality of humanity's utter dependence on the mercy of God. This prayer rightly places all of the power in the hands of God to do with his creation as he pleases. The penitent prays that God would act according to his great mercy and do the necessary work of remaking his creation to be conformed to the image of the Son.

In each of these prayers, Anselm focuses on the mercy of God reaching into the life of unworthy sinners. He consistently prays—and has his readers pray alongside him—that God would act in the individual's life according to his unique wisdom. These prayers remain focused not only on the provisions that God alone can bring but also on the necessity of God's work in ordering the life of the sinner—both physically and spiritually.

Sources

50–55: Gabriel Gerberon, ed., *Sancti Anselmi Ex Beccensi Abbate Cantuariensis Archiepiscopi Opera: Nec Non Eadmeri Monachi Cantuariensis Historia Novorum, Et Alia Opuscula*, 2nd ed (Paris: Sumptibus Montalant, 1721), 30, 35, 244–45, 255, 261, 263.

56: Martin Rule, ed., *St. Anselm's Book of Meditations and Prayers* (London: M. R., 1872), 89–90.

❧ 22. Bonaventure (1221–1274)

Bonaventure (born Giovanni di Fidanza) studied at the University of Paris as a Franciscan friar. He was a contemporary of Thomas Aquinas and served as a public defender of the Franciscans, ultimately being elected minister general of the Franciscan order. He was closely connected with the Franciscan pope, Gregory X, who elevated Bonaventure to the cardinalate. At the end of Bonaventure's life, he attended the Second Council of Lyon at the behest of the pope. At the council, Bonaventure played a pivotal role in obtaining the short-lived reunion of the Greek and Latin churches before he died suddenly in 1274. Some scholars have suggested that he was assassinated, but this suspicion has never been proven.

During his writing career, Bonaventure produced a commentary on Lombard's *Sentences*, an influential commentary on Luke's Gospel, and several works about the Christian life. He has been recognized as one of the major philosophers of the medieval church and was given the title "doctor of the church" by Pope Sixtus V in 1587.

For the most part, Bonaventure's theology falls within the broader Augustinian tradition. He focused especially on connecting theology to the affections of the heart rather than only to the intellect. But Bonaventure was not opposed to intellectual pursuits. He entered into the major philosophical-theological arguments of his day, proving himself an adept student of Augustine and Anselm, among others. His logical proof for God combined with his understanding of the human condition (including humanity's inherent longing for joy) left a legacy that continues to bear fruit.

"I have not yet expressed or even begun to understand" stems from Bonaventure's personal reflection on the theological writings of Anselm. In fact, the prayer includes a lengthy quotation from Bonaventure's copy of Anselm's work. The original can be found in Bonaventure's *Breviloquium* (*Brief Reading*), which served as a short overview of his theology.

The second prayer included in our volume is a modernized version of a prayer from a seventeenth-century English edition of Bonaventure's *Soliloquium de quatuor mentalibus exercitiis* (*Soliloquy on the Four Spiritual Exercises*), a devotional guide intended to be used by the Franciscan order. This prayer ("Let us bow the knees of our heart") serves as a call to worship, focusing on an intense longing for God and the holy devotion that leads to knowing him and experiencing his joy.

Sources

57: A. C. Peltier, ed., *S. R. E. Cardinalis S. Bonaventurae Ex Ordine Minorum Episcopi Albanensis, Eximii Ecclesiae Doctoris Opera Omnia* (Paris: Ludovicus Vivès, 1864), 7:343.

58: Bonaventure, *The Soliloquies of St. Bonaventure Containing His Four Mental Exercises and Also His Treatise Called, a Bundle of Myrrh, Concerning the Passion of Our Saviour: With xii Spirituall Exercises of the Said St. Bonaventure* (London, 1655), A11r.

⮞ 23. Thomas Aquinas (1225–1274)

Born to a noble family in Aquino, Italy, Thomas Aquinas was expected to enter a life of service to the church, probably as a successor to his paternal uncle Sinibald who was abbot of the Benedictine monastery at Monte Cassino. His education took him to the newly established university at Naples and he ultimately determined to join the Dominican order. Aquinas's willingness to accept the vows of poverty required by the Dominicans did not sit well with his family, and they tried to convince him to change his plans. Aquinas, however, remained resolute in his commitment and eventually joined the Dominicans in 1244.

Aquinas's initial assignment in the Order included studying at the University of Paris under the tutelage of the Dominican scholar Albert the Great. Aquinas followed Albert to Cologne in 1248 where Aquinas was named master student despite his unusual proclivity for silence. When Aquinas's peers doubted his abilities, labeling him a "dumb ox," Albert reportedly defended Aquinas's ability by warning the other students,

"We call him the dumb ox, but he will make resound in his doctrine such a bellowing that it will echo throughout the entire world."[2] That warning proved to be prophetic of Aquinas's voluminous writings, which included biblical commentaries, an influential commentary on Peter Lombard's *Sentences*, polemical works, and complex philosophical arguments. By far his most important work, the *Summa theologiae,* was intended to be an introductory work for novices, an aim Aquinas took seriously as the master of the University of Paris from 1268 to 1272. In 1272, Aquinas received permission to establish an institute of learning in any place he desired and he decided to do so in Naples. He soon began work on the third and final section of the *Summa*. A mystical experience in December 1273 (one of several he reported in his life) left Aquinas determined to stop writing, declaring to his assistant, "I cannot [write] any more. Everything I have written seems to me as straw in comparison with what I have seen."[3]

Despite his work being well-received and even being commissioned directly by the pope for a work on the disagreement between the East and the West (which became *Contra errores Graecorum* or *Against the Errors of the Greeks*), Aquinas's

2   Torrell, Jean-Pierre, Robert Royal, Matthew K. Minerd, and Jean-Pierre Torrell, *Saint Thomas Aquinas* (Piraí: Catholic University of America Press, 2005), 1:26.

3   Torrell et al., *Saint Thomas Aquinas*, 1:289.

writings still sparked debate. For example, the bishop of Paris published official condemnations of Aquinas's work in 1270 and again in 1277 (after Aquinas's death). Despite that condemnation, Aquinas's work became the foundation of theological training for later generations, with a copy of his *Summa* being placed alongside the Bible at the Council of Trent late in the sixteenth century. Pope Pius V also named Aquinas a doctor of the church.

The prayers included in our volume come from a variety of Aquinas's writings. Most have appeared in various collections in the centuries since Aquinas's death. On the whole, they focus on the divine activity that results in a sinner being conformed to the holy image of the Son, recognizing that no one can do this by their own will. Aquinas offers prayers for all readers and specifically for students, all the while praying for himself as well.

"Grant to me, oh merciful God, that I may wholeheartedly desire" asks God to help keep oneself focused on righteous goals so that the allure of the temporary would not overwhelm the righteous desires for the eternal. The Latin text demonstrates Aquinas's mastery of the language. Certainly, no translation can do complete justice to this wordsmith's work, but the current translation aims to provide some glimpse of both his eloquence and his godly desire.

In "Ineffable Creator," Aquinas turns his attention to his students. He starts the prayer by noting God's role in the creation of the angels, specifically their ordering. This reflects Aquinas's unique teaching that he gave to his students about the ranks and hierarchies of angels. Even without that portion, however, the prayer provides incredible insight from a teacher who longed for his students to grow in their knowledge, understanding, and ability. It is meant to be prayed by a student before the beginning of any new lesson.

In "I praise, glorify, and bless you," Aquinas attempts to express the inexpressible, to put words to the task of acknowledging God's awe-inspiring care for his people. Our new translation from the Latin aims to capture the poetic nature of the prayer while still making it understandable to the modern reader. This particular prayer has been accepted as part of the Aquinas corpus since at least the nineteenth century, though some doubts remain as to its authenticity. Regardless, it provides words for powerful feelings of gratitude to the God who is worthy of praise.

Sources

59–60: Ambrose St. John, ed., *The Raccolta, or a Collection of Indulgenced Prayers and Good Works* (London: Burns and Oates, 1910), 33, 177.

61: Stanislas Edouard Fretté and Paul Maré, eds, *Doctoris Angelici Divi Thomae Aquinatis Sacri Ordinis F. F. Praedicatorum Opera Omnia: Sive Antehac Excusa, Sive Etiam Anecdota* (Parisiis: Apud Ludovicum Vivès, 1871), 32:821.

❧ 24. Thomas Bradwardine (ca. 1290–1349)

Thomas Bradwardine served for the better part of two months as the archbishop of Canterbury (4 June 1349–26 August 1349) at the end of his short life and storied career. He had been educated at Balliol College, Oxford, before becoming a fellow of Merton College. During his time at the University of Oxford, he served as professor of divinity and as a confessor to Edward III. In the end, he received numerous degrees from Oxford: a BA by 1321, MA by 1323, BTh by 1333, and DTh by 1348.

Bradwardine had a high view of God's sovereignty, which was seen by many as being heavily influenced by Augustine and pitted him regularly against other philosopher-theologians such as his Oxford colleague William of Ockham. In fact, Bradwardine's most famous work, *De causa Dei contra Pelagium et de virtute causarum* (*On the Cause of God Against the Pelagians and on the Virtue of that Cause*) directly recalled the fifth-century controversy between Augustine and Pelagius.

In addition, Bradwardine published numerous works dealing with natural theology, mathematics, and mnemonics, ultimately earning the title "profound doctor" from the Pope. As a leading academic in the English church and an ambassador of the English crown on numerous occasions, Bradwardine's theological positions made headway across the continent and in the British Isles. His work on predestination and the doctrines of grace greatly influenced John Wycliffe, who was also associated with Merton College, Oxford.

The prayer "My God, I love you above all else" can be found in The Book of Private Devotions, which was collected by an English cleric and published in 1839. The prayer's focus on God himself (rather than his blessings) being the greatest gift of all provides a clear indication of Bradwardine's spiritual devotion, or at least the devotion he desired for himself.

Source

62: Edward Bickersteth, ed., *The Book of Private Devotions; Containing a Collection of Early Devotions of the Reformers and Their Successors in the English Church* (London, 1839), 245.

25. Thomas à Kempis (1380–1471)

Thomas served as a canon regular in the fifteenth century and was known for his devotional writing and personal discipline of copying Scripture. The English form of his name is erroneously derived from the Latin name of his hometown (Kempis). Interestingly, the accented form of *a* has no meaning in Latin, but for some reason, that version has stuck.

During his early years, Thomas became associated with the Brethren of the Common Life, a religious lay society focused on providing religious education for laity and authentic spiritual reform amid a perceived nominal Christianity. Numerous theologians of the later Middle Ages were counted among their pupils, including Gabriel Biel, Martin Luther, and Desiderius Erasmus.

The Brethren of the Common Life focused on providing spiritual works for their students as part of a movement that came to be known as the *devotio moderna* (modern devotion), and Thomas adopted the cause as his own even though he had finished his education. This spiritual movement focused less on the rituals of the church and more on the personal, spiritual devotion of the individual with the aim of engendering an immersive devotion to God in both secular and ecclesial vocations.

During his adult years, Thomas's reputation for spiritual writing continued to develop, and he eventually took on a leadership role in a monastery at Mount Saint Agnes in Zwolle, Netherlands, having joined the Augustinian order in 1406. Thomas copied the Bible in its entirety at least four times during his life while also writing a host of other works, including multiple commentaries, sermons aimed to help new members of the monastery, and personal devotional works.

A collection of smaller writings ultimately became his most famous work, *Imitatio Christi* (*The Imitation of Christ*). Completed by 1427, *Imitatio Christi* quickly became popular, in part because of its close chronological proximity to the invention of the moveable type printing press. The first printed edition of the work arrived on the scene in 1471, and by the middle of the seventeenth century, more than seven hundred editions had been published.

The work was originally published anonymously, following the teaching of the author that notoriety should not be the aim of the authentic follower of Christ. Yet, despite the stated desire for anonymity, the work became associated with Thomas quite quickly, and a 1441 autograph identified him as the author. His authorship is not in question. Other than the Bible itself, perhaps no other book had a greater legacy for several centuries. By the end of the fifteenth century, *Imitatio Christi* had been translated into at least eight different languages, and several English versions followed soon after the beginning of the sixteenth century. Scholars have identified at least two thousand different published editions of the work. According to several sources, *Imitatio Christi* remains the most translated Christian work apart from the Bible.

The prayers included in our volume come from various early English editions of Thomas's writings. These English editions often carried disparate titles, but they were generally either new translations or new paraphrases of the original Latin work of Thomas. These prayers were chosen for their focus on the holiness of God and the deep longing for God that is rightly felt by all who would follow him but also for their diction, which complements the heart of the author.

"Oh most sweet and loving Lord" is a modernized rendition of a prayer from a seventeenth-century English devotional entitled *The Christians Pattern or the Imitation of Christ* (1677). This work presented an abridged English version of Thomas à Kempis's writings from two centuries prior. In it, the reader can hear and echo Thomas's passionate desire for a personal devotion to God.

The fourth section of Thomas's *Imitatio Christi* formed the basis of a late sixteenth-century English work entitled *Soliloquium Animae.* Thomas Rogers purported to present the first published English translation. In the prayer included in our volume ("Your eyes saw me even before I was formed"), Thomas à Kempis prays to the omnipotent God who understands humanity's shortcomings and notes his own inability to follow through on personal resolutions. Ultimately, Thomas realizes his utter despair. This lengthy section gives words to his recognition of the fleeting nature of earthly joys and the deceptive nature of human desires.

"Let me understand the shortness of my days" turns one's attention to eternity as Thomas reminds himself (and his reader) that the temporal things of this earth are fleeting; they do not deserve the attention and devotion they are often given. Ultimately, in spite of all the troubles he faced, Thomas reminds himself—and begs God to continue reminding him—of God's goodness and protection.

Sources

63: Thomas à Kempis, *The Christians Pattern, or, a Divine Treatise of the Imitation of Christ* (London, 1677), 319.

64–65: Thomas Rogers, *Soliloquium Animae. The Sole-Talke of the Soule* [. . .] (London, 1592), 25–29, 35–36.

7

Reformation Church
(1500–1700)

❧ 26. Martin Luther (1483–1546)

Known preeminently for his role in the Protestant Reformation, Martin Luther was an Augustinian friar who was ordained as a minister in 1507. He initially followed his father's
wishes and studied law at the University of Erfurt. However,
his true interests lay in the larger questions about life, so the
young Martin eventually entered the Augustinian monastery at Erfurt and began a formal study of theology. Here,
he came under the supervision of Johann von Staupitz who
served both as Luther's confessor and as the superior of the
monastery. Staupitz soon made a move to the new University
of Wittenberg as a professor and head of the theology faculty

and he took Luther with him both to serve on the faculty and continue his academic study of theology.

During his time at Wittenberg (from 1508 until his death in 1546), Luther became increasingly convinced of the need for major reforms within the church. His understanding of the righteousness of God and salvation by faith alone quickly became battle cries for those within the church who understood the need for clearer doctrinal teaching, moral improvement, and higher standards of pastoral care. Thanks to the use of the newly developed moveable type printing press, Luther's ideas spread across Europe and eventually led to the cataclysmic shift in the ecclesiastical landscape known as the Reformation.

Throughout that fight, Luther saw himself as a pastor. His initial foray into perceived rebellion against the church of Rome came in the form of his *Ninety-Five Theses*, a document intended to protest the abuse of the poor parishioners of Wittenberg through (what he believed to be) the unbiblical practice of the sale of indulgences. As he continued down the long journey toward complete separation from Rome, Luther maintained his concern for those under his care, ruler and peasant alike, and all those in between. He also continued to grow in his own personal faith journey, which led him not only to consider deeper questions of theology (as seen, for example, in his fight with other Reformers over the nature of the elements of the Lord's Supper) but also to develop a deep appreciation for assurance of salvation in Christ. His many devotional works, hymns, and catechisms provide a glimpse into this lifelong journey.

Overall, Luther left behind a massive written record and had a significant impact on the Western world. In fact, many have reported that more has been written on Martin Luther than any other figure in Western history other than Jesus Christ.

The prayers from Luther's hand that have been selected for our volume ("Behold, Lord, I am an empty vessel" and "Oh my dear Lord Jesus Christ, you know the poor condition of my soul") are new translations of the original German versions. They demonstrate Luther's understanding of the human condition, which was at the core of his early theological shifts. Luther's exploration of Augustine's understanding of the same topic and Luther's incorporation of the effects of original sin into his theological reading of Scripture can be seen in these personal prayers that expose the core of his struggles and the only reason for his hope.

Sources

66: *Sommerpostille 1526, Matthew 9:18-26*, Weimarer Ausgabe 10.2.438.

67: *Das beicht gebett. D. Martini Lutther*, Weimarer Ausgabe 48.275.

❧ 27. Martin Bucer (1491–1551)

Counted among the first generation of Protestant Reformers, Martin Bucer spent most of his ministerial life in Strasbourg working alongside other well-known theologians like Wolfgang Capito (1478–1541) until the political climate forced him to leave. In his final years, he served as regius professor of divinity at the University of Cambridge. In that role, he worked alongside Thomas Cranmer, the archbishop of Canterbury, to oversee the theological establishment of the Edwardian church.

Bucer must have received a decent education because he entered the Dominican order in 1507 and soon began studying theology at the University of Heidelberg. Heidelberg was the site of the famous Heidelberg Disputation where Martin Luther defended his theology. Bucer attended the Disputation and became convinced of Luther's major theological positions.

Bucer's positions and those of the Dominican order became increasingly difficult to hold in tension, and Bucer eventually gained his release from his vows in 1521. He signaled a full break with Rome when he married a former nun in the summer of 1522. He was determined to study in Wittenburg under Luther, but his journey was delayed when he accepted a position as chaplain to a Reformer in Wissenbourg, where he stayed until his excommunication from the Roman church made him an outlaw in May 1523. From there, he turned to Strassbourg to support the Reformation as well as the unification of the Protestant cause until his final move to Cambridge in 1549.

As is befitting of a man with a career in the church and academia, Bucer left a legacy of numerous works that were translated and published throughout Europe both during and after his life. He explored his vision for the Christian life in a work entitled *De Regno Christi* and also worked extensively on Cranmer's new Book of Common Prayer.

The prayer included in our volume ("Oh Lord God and heavenly Father") is taken from a book published in England more than a decade after Bucer's death, which demonstrates his continuing legacy. The prayer stems from an explication of Matthew 18, especially its description of the temptation to desire earthly gains. The same magnetism of fame and fortune that threatened to sidetrack the disciples also reared its ugly head for Bucer and his contemporaries, as it does for us today, thus making this prayer still relevant to modern readers.

Source

68: Martin Bucer, preface to *The Mynd and Exposition Of. . . Martyn Bucer Uppon These Wordes of S. Mathew* [. . .] (Emden, 1566).

✺ 28. Thomas Cranmer (1489–1556)

Caught in the middle of the political turmoil that character-ized sixteenth-century England, Thomas Cranmer found himself squarely in the spotlight. He rose to prominence during the crisis surrounding Henry VIII's attempt to have his first marriage annulled. Cranmer—at that point a fellow at Jesus College, Cambridge, where he had previously received his bachelor's and master's degrees—assisted the king's chief counselor, Thomas Cardinal Wolsey, in that case. During his time working on the annulment, Cranmer developed close relationships with many leading Reformers including Bucer, Zwingli, Oecolampadius, and Osiander, even marrying into Osiander's family.

With some behind-the-scenes help from the family of Anne Boleyn, the soon-to-be queen, Thomas Cranmer was named archbishop of Canterbury in 1532 despite not holding high positions in the church before then. While archbishop, Cranmer served as one of Henry's leading counselors as they finalized the split with Rome. Cranmer found himself caught up in the back-and-forth of the newly formed Church of En-gland wherein some gains were made by Reformers and others by the traditionalists. Cranmer himself became convinced of the Protestant cause and ultimately installed several continen-tal Reformers in professorships at Oxford and Cambridge.

After the death of Henry VIII, Cranmer took the opportunity to ensure that the Church of England would be firmly established in its Protestant theology, a task made easier by his role in overseeing the education of Edward VI before his accession to the throne. Cranmer also oversaw the production of the Forty-two Articles (1553) and the first version of the Book of Common Prayer (1549), which together formed the doctrinal standards for the Edwardian church. Unfortunately for Cranmer, Edward's reign was short-lived. Edward's eventual successor, the Catholic Mary I, had Cranmer arrested and eventually executed in Oxford in 1556.

During his sixty-seven years, Cranmer published regularly. His works include liturgies, statements of faith, correspondence with major thinkers of the age, and sermons. Having been executed as a heretic, his works risked being lost to oblivion, but when Mary I died and the Protestant Elizabeth I ascended to the throne, Cranmer's work regained its place of honor. His Forty-two Articles even served as the basis for the Elizabethan Thirty-Nine Articles, and his version of the prayer book became increasingly popular.

The prayers included in our volume come from that Edwardian Book of Common Prayer and are thus intended for communal use of the faithful. "Almighty God, give us grace" calls for God to help with defenses against the "works of darkness." "Blessed Lord, who has caused all Holy Scriptures to be written" turns the congregation's attention to the Holy Spirit's work through Scripture.

Source

69–70: *The Common Prayer and Ordinal* (1549), vii, v, xi v.

✎ 29. John Calvin (1509–1564)

Of all the sixteenth-century Reformers, only Martin Luther has garnered more attention in the succeeding generations than John Calvin. As a refugee from Catholic France, Calvin spent some time in Basel and Strasbourg but made his greatest impact in Geneva, where he worked alongside Guillaume Farel to bring reform.

The steps toward becoming a leader of the Reformation were not easily discernible in Calvin's early life. His mother died while he was young, and his father determined that he would study law despite (or maybe because of) his academic prowess in his early studies in philosophy. Yet, Calvin's shift to law and corresponding move to the University of Orléans did not stifle his theological inquiry. Eventually (no later than 1533), Calvin experienced what he called a conversion after receiving a taste of true godliness. The resulting fervor from that experience would empower his ministry for the remainder of his days.

In 1533, Calvin found himself on the radar of the Catholic establishment, in large part because of his close connection with the rector of the University of Paris, Nicolas Cop, who was an early leader in the call for French reform. After Cop made his position official in his inaugural address, both he and Calvin (who may have written that address) were forced into exile. In the initial stages of that exile, Calvin published the first edition of what would become his most famous work, *Institutio Christianae Religionis* (*Institutes of the Christian Religion*).

After some initial stops in various cities, including Basel, Calvin was convinced by Farel to aid in the reforming work in Geneva. Their work was not without controversy and even led to a period of exile for the two reformers. Calvin returned to Geneva in 1541 and remained there until his death in 1564, installing the plans he and Farel had devised in their early days of cooperation. By the end of his life, Calvin had established an ecclesiastical structure that oversaw the spiritual formation of the people of Geneva. He published a liturgical handbook, a catechism, a host of theological treatises, sermons, and commentaries, and five editions of his magnum opus, the *Institutes*.

While in Geneva, he preached more than two thousand sermons—multiple times on Sundays and once on most weekdays. Yet, his legacy reached far beyond that city. His theological system has become synonymous with a particular brand of Protestant Reformed teaching, largely because of the immense success of his teaching ministry both personally and through the work of his students in the church and at the Academy of Geneva, a theological school that eventually became the University of Geneva. Calvin's successful missions program—which sent dedicated missionaries to France, the Netherlands, Hungary, and even the Americas—led to strongholds of Calvinistic doctrine across the world. Additionally, Geneva became a major center of refuge for Protestants, including those fleeing the persecution of Mary I in England, and the systems established in Geneva were used as a model for later systems of reform work in the refugees' home countries, such as Scotland. Calvin also worked hard to unite and galvanize the Protestant cause across different countries. Through all of this, Calvin was first and foremost a pastor, responsible for the spiritual formation of his flock.

The prayers included in our volume come from some of Calvin's works of collected prayers as well as his sermons and commentaries on biblical texts. "My God, my Father and Preserver" asks God for help in the performing of the mundane.

For Calvin, the mundane tasks could be either an opportunity to worship or to become overwhelmed by sin. This prayer reminds his flock that they need God to protect them from the latter and to assist them in achieving the former. "Oh Lord, fountain of all wisdom and learning" is specifically intended for students, probably for use in the formal educational activity of the Academy, but it also speaks to anyone who is still learning about God. The other two prayers from Calvin's pen ("Almighty God, since at the coming of Christ, your Son" and "Almighty God, since we have already entered in hope") stem from his lectures on two different passages of Scripture (Micah 4 and Ezekiel 20 respectively). These would have been prayed at the end of Calvin's lectures on the biblical texts, which included detailed exegesis. "Almighty God, since we have already entered in hope" was the prayer offered at the end of what would be his final lecture.

Sources

71–72; John Calvin, *Tracts Relating to the Reformation*, ed. Henry Beveridge (Edinburgh: Calvin Translation Society, 1844), 2: 95–97

73: John Calvin, *Commentaries on the Twelve Minor Prophets by John Calvin*, trans. John Owen (Edinburgh: Calvin Translation Society, 1847), 268.

74: John Calvin, *Commentaries on the First Twenty Chapters of the Book of the Prophet Ezekiel by John Calvin*, trans. Thomas Meyers (Edinburgh: Calvin Translation Society, 1850), 345.

❧ 30. Henry Bull (d. ca. 1577)

Henry Bull was removed from the University of Oxford after Mary I had ascended to the throne. His stance in defense of Edwardian Protestantism left him and a group of his colleagues at Magdalen College in clear opposition to the crown. Whether Bull went into exile or merely avoided persecution by staying at his home in Warwickshire is unknown, but he rose to prominence after Elizabeth I gained the throne in 1558. He received several positions in the Elizabethan church and also worked on various publications. He almost certainly helped John Foxe, his colleague and friend from Oxford, on Foxe's famous martyrology. Further, he edited the *Apology* of Bishop John Hooper, the Marian martyr, and worked on a translation of Martin Luther's *Commentary on the Psalms*. Bull also published several collections of prayers, including *Lidley's Prayers* (1566) and *Christian Praiers and Holy Meditacions* (1570). The former has caused some consternation for scholars because the identity of Lidley remains a mystery. Some have suggested that this was a misprint for Ludlow, who is listed in the stationer's registry, but this is mere speculation.

At any rate, Bull is responsible for collecting these prayers into a useful handbook for his readership.

Christian Praiers is the source for the two prayers included in our volume. In "There is nothing, oh Lord, more like your holy nature than a quiet mind," Bull rues the distracting noise of the world, whether it comes from people, trials and tribulations, or even the weather. He desires to enjoy "a godly quietness" so that he can also become righteous. "You know, oh Lord, what is most profitable and expedient for me" is a lengthier prayer that echoes this sentiment and asks God to intervene in the lives of believers lest the common temptations of humanity overwhelm them and their small desires for righteousness.

Source

75–76: Henry Bull, *Christian Praiers and Holie Meditations as Wel for Priuate as Publique Exercise* [. . .] (London, 1578), 155–56, 365–66.

✎ 31. Lancelot Andrewes (1555–1626)

As a prominent church leader during the reigns of Elizabeth I and James I, the Cambridge-educated Lancelot Andrewes made a name for himself as both a biblical scholar and a spokesperson for the moderating Anglican position that would become the foundation for the future Church of England. Andrewes preached regularly to the court of James I, especially on significant anniversaries such as that of the Gunpowder Plot. He was among the best rhetoricians of his era, and Charles I requested the publication of a lengthy collection of his sermons in the years following his death. His oratorical skills were so excellent that he developed a large following, especially in the literary world.

As a biblical scholar, Andrewes found himself in a position of great influence at a providentially significant moment. He participated in the coronation of James I as king of England and soon after participated in the Hampton Court Conference (1604). Andrewes then took on a lead role in the translation and production of the King James Version of the Bible, itself a result of the negotiations surrounding the Hampton Court Conference. He served as the head of the First Westminster Company of translators, and his name appears at the top of the list of translators (incidentally, his brother Roger also served on a translation team for the King James Bible).

In addition to Andrewes's sermons, he also published a large number of polemical works, catechetical works, ministerial handbooks, and devotionals. His writings have been collected into several different anthologies, with one that runs to eleven volumes. Of all Andrewes's works, the one that had the widest reception was *The Private Devotions of the Right Reverend Father in God Lancelot Andrewes.* This book, published posthumously, provided helpful insight into the everyday theology of Andrewes. The prayers included in our volume come from a later edition of *Private Devotions.*

Both of these prayers ("Give me grace, oh Lord" and "From all innovations, private interpretations, minor differences in doctrine") stem from Andrewes own struggle with humanity's sinful nature. He understands, both from theological consideration and from personal experience, that humanity is incapable of righting itself. Humans need God to restrain them from wandering away from the paths of righteousness. Additionally, as a minister in an intensely divided church, Andrewes recognizes the dangers that sinfulness poses to the church as a whole. So, in both prayers, he asks for God to act on behalf of his people, begging him to make unrighteousness difficult so that they would not be dissuaded from true desire, true affections, and the true God.

Source

77–78: Lancelot Andrewes, *The Private Devotions of the Right Reverend Father in God Lancelot Andrewes* [. . .] (London, 1647), 48–50, 69–71.

❧ 32. George Webbe (1581–1642)

George Webbe studied at Oxford, first at New College and then transferring to Corpus Christi, where he earned a BA in 1602 and an MA in 1605. After receiving a DD in 1624, he served as a chaplain to Charles I in the early part of Charles's reign, even baptizing the king's firstborn son (who died in infancy). The controversial Archbishop of Canterbury William Laud saw to Webb's appointment as bishop of Limerick in 1634, and Webbe served there during the Catholic uprising of 1641. He died at King John's Castle in Limerick in 1642 while it was being besieged by Catholic forces.

Before his arrival at Limerick, Webb enjoyed a prolific writing ministry, publishing theological treatises, devotionals, and several series of sermons between 1609 and 1619. His most popular work focused on the spiritual life of the Christian. That book, entitled *The Practice of Quietnes,* went through at least seven editions by the time he was consecrated as bishop.

The lengthy prayer included in our volume is taken from Webbe's book-length work on the compiler of Proverbs 30, Agur, the son of Jakeh. In this book, entitled *Agur's Prayer, or, The Christians Choyce, for the Outward Estate and Condition of This Present Life,* Webbe outlines the middle ground between the poor person's preoccupation with finding resources and the rich person's obsession with wealth. The prayer itself ("Oh Lord

God, who is infinite in greatness, power, glory, and majesty") gives voice to the believers who find themselves in a situation of relative wealth. This surely serves as an autobiographical prayer as Webbe experienced relative wealth in his positions in the Church of England, but the prayer also speaks to many of those living in the West today.

Source

79: George Webbe, *Agurs Prayer; or, the Christians Choyce, for the Outward Estate and Condition of This Present Life* (London, 1621), 342–48.

❧ 33. Jeremy Taylor (1613–1667)

Jeremy Taylor was a close confidante of William Laud, Charles I's archbishop of Canterbury, and fell under the suspicious eye of parliament as the country moved toward civil war. Taylor had been a chaplain in ordinary to Charles I thanks to Laud's support. After gaining the attention of the establishment during his studies at Gonville and Caius College, Cambridge, Taylor eventually received a fellowship at All Souls College, Oxford.

After the onset of the civil wars, Taylor removed himself to Wales in order to live a relatively quiet life after being imprisoned at least three separate times for his royalist connections.

Upon the restoration of the Stuart monarchy, Taylor was installed as bishop of Down and Connor in Ireland, a position he held until his death. He also served as vice-chancellor of Trinity College Dublin at the University of Dublin. During the interregnum, Taylor advanced his writing career, eventually gaining significant notoriety. His work included everything from multiple collections of sermons to theological treatises and devotionals and manuals for prayer. Taylor's works have generally not gone out of print, with a lengthy collection of them being published in the nineteenth century and many of his seventeenth-century publications now becoming available in digital collections.

"You have called me to open my hand so that you can fill it" begs God for help, noting that the believer cannot even desire rightly without God's influence. "Eternal God, sweetest Jesus" turns one's attention to Christ's amazing willingness to endure maltreatment at the hands of his creation. Taylor begs God to allow that passion to be enflamed in him so that he can love God righteously. The remainder of Taylor's prayers in this collection come from his devotional work, *The Rule and Exercises of Holy Living* (1650). Those prayers (including "Fix my thoughts, my hopes, and my desires upon heaven," "Teach me to watch over all my ways," "Let no riches ever allow me to forget who I am," "Oh eternal and gracious Father, you have set marriage apart as a holy mystery," "Oh Lord God of infinite mercy and infinite excellence," "Oh eternal God, Father of mercies and God of all comfort," "Oh holy Jesus, King of the saints and Prince of the universal church") collectively teach readers to set their eyes on God in all aspects of life. Taylor reminds them to beg God for help, especially in the mundane aspects of life. He also reminds them of the ever-present dangers associated with the allure of wealth, the reality of a disunified church, and the constant struggle to maintain the sanctity of marriage.

Sources

80: Jeremy Taylor, *The Worthy Communicant* [. . .] (London, 1661), 555.

81: Jeremy Taylor and William Cave, *Antiquitates Christianae: Or, the History of the Life and Death of the Holy Jesus* [. . .] (London, 1675), 388.

82–88: Jeremy Taylor, *The Rule and Exercises of Holy Living* [. . .] (London, 1650), 46–47, 52, 176–77, 360–63, 397.

❧ 34. Henry Scougal (1650–1678)

Despite dying at the young age of twenty-eight, Henry Scougal left an amazing legacy. Henry was born into a religious family (his father Patrick was the bishop of Aberdeen) and thus received a solid biblical education in his youth. At the age of fifteen, he matriculated at the University of Aberdeen, where he spent the rest of his life, except for one year, which he spent as a pastor in a village outside of Aberdeen.

Shortly after graduating from the University, Scougal was appointed professor of divinity at his alma mater, a position he would hold until his untimely death in June 1678 due to complications from consumption. Despite dying at such an early age, Scougal left behind an important collection of writings that included sermons, essays, a textbook on moral philosophy, and treatises on pastoral theology.

The prayer included in our volume ("Most gracious God") comes from his most famous work, *The Life of God in the Soul of Man*, published in 1677 and originally written as a defense of Christianity for a friend. The work was immediately well-received, reaching a fifty-nine editions by 1800. Those significantly influenced by Scougal's apology for Christianity included Gilbert Burnet—the famous historian, church leader, and propagandist of William's and Mary's reigns—as well as leading figures of the eighteenth-century Great Awakening. In fact, John Wesley abridged one of the editions of Scougal's work and George Whitefield funded its publication. The prayer in our volume is the last one included in Wesley's edition and serves as a concluding benediction for Scougal's friend and later readers.

Source

89: Henry Scougal, *The Life of God in the Soul of Man* [. . .] (London, 1677), 126–28.

➥ 35. John Kettlewell (1653–1695)

In the short forty-two years of his life, this Oxford-educated (St Edmund Hall) minister made significant waves. He engaged numerous theological disputes, including the relationship between the church and the crown, even as the Glorious Revolution (1688–1689) took place around him. Kettlewell left a fellowship at Lincoln College, Oxford, in 1683 and focused on parish ministry in Warwickshire. Shortly thereafter, he married Jane Lybb.

During the entirety of his married life, Kettlewell focused on parish ministry and his writing career, publishing devotionals, sermons, and polemical works. His pen gained him enough of a reputation to land him a position as chaplain to the Countess of Bedford, but that same pen also garnered a healthy dose of suspicion from the new administration. Kettlewell died at his home in London, where he had moved after being deprived of his pastoral position.

Apart from his political works, his writings—largely consisting of sermons and prayers—were well-received throughout his life. The two prayers included in our volume ("I give you my heart" and "Let me have your peace, oh gracious Father!") focus on the personal experience of the penitent. These prayers can be found in Kettlewell's devotional work entitled *A Companion for the Penitent* (1694) and put words to his desire to find peace and comfort only in the one true, living God. Kettlewell asks God not to allow his experience of God's mercy to result in any sort of abuse of that mercy or even in taking it for granted and reminds himself of his dependence on God to avoid things that are detrimental to his soul or dangerous to godly living.

Source

90–91: John Kettlewell, *A Companion for the Penitent* [. . .] (London, 1694), 28–29, 37–38.

8

Modern Church
(1700–1900)

⮞ 36. Isaac Watts (1674–1748)

Isaac Watts is best known as an English hymnwriter and theologian in the English Dissenting tradition. By the age of thirteen, he learned Latin, Greek, French, and Hebrew, and later in life he turned down a university education because it would have required him to conform to the Church of England. He first took up hymn writing to address the apathetic singing he perceived within his church. Folklore suggests that when he noted this to his father, his father recommended writing better songs to sing. In the end, Isaac wrote over six hundred hymns, and many are still sung in churches today, including "When I Survey the

Wondrous Cross," "Joy to the World," and "O God, Our Help in Ages Past."

Watts's life was not without controversy. His greatest contribution to hymnody was the conviction that a New Testament interpretation of the Psalms should be adapted for modern congregations. In fact, many of his most popular hymns do just this. For example, "Joy to the World" follows Psalm 98 and highlights the life, death, and resurrection of Jesus Christ. This approach was not universally appreciated during his time, but many evangelicals continue to benefit from Watts's pious hymns.

Watts also authored a book of set prayers that he hoped would provide a similar benefit to that of his hymns. He believed that young children would especially benefit from having model prayers that they could imitate in order to learn how to pray on their own. His 1728 *Prayers Composed for the Use and Imitation of Children* was divided into sections for young children, adolescents, and adults. The work contained set prayers for evenings, mornings, and special occasions. "Oh Lord God who is most high and most holy" models an ideal prayer's scope and sequence, moving the heart through adoration, confession, petition, and thanksgiving.

Source

92: Isaac Watts, *Prayers Composed for the Use and Imitation of Children* [. . .] (London, 1728), 40–45.

37. Samuel Johnson (1709–1784)

Samuel Johnson was a titan of the eighteenth century, leaving a legacy as a poet, playwright, moralist, editor, and lexicographer. He studied at Pembroke College, Oxford, where he authored poems and verse, some of which he would later publish in *Miscellany* (1733). Johnson's *Dictionary of the English Language* established the authority of dictionaries as prescriptive reference works at a time when the spelling, grammar, and syntax of English was influenced more by common usage in the liturgy of the church and the broader societal culture than by a standard system. His dictionary included memorable definitions, fixed pronunciations for words, and illustrative quotations.

As a devout Anglican, Johnson also authored dozens of sermons and prayers. However, these have not garnered the same attention as his dictionary or essays. The prayer included in our volume was originally published posthumously in *Prayers and Meditations*. Many of its prayers were marked by Johnson's familiarity with physical suffering and grieving the death of loved ones. Biographers believe Johnson was afflicted with gout and probably had Tourette's syndrome, but his fame as a scholar and critic during his lifetime overshadowed his affliction, which was only recorded in personal documents. Only in posthumous publications did readers see his pleas for God to comfort him and show mercy to his deceased family members. "Almighty and most merciful Father" is one of the prayers Johnson wrote as he contemplated his despair over the death of his wife and got ready for church on Easter Sunday. This prayer encapsulates the reality that in life on this side of heaven, the Christian is "always sorrowful and rejoicing."

Source

93: Samuel Johnson and George Strahan, *Prayers and Meditations*, 2nd ed. (London, 1785), 157–58.

❧ 38. John Wesley (1703–1791)

John Wesley is best remembered for his work in establishing pious reform societies within the Church of England. John, his brother Charles, and George Whitefield were members of one such holy club during their time at Christ Church, Oxford, in the mid-1720s. Later, John had a powerful spiritual experience, feeling his "heart strangely warmed" during the preaching of the pietistic Moravian Christians.[1] The subse-

1 John Wesley, *The Works of John Wesley*, 3rd ed. (London: Wesleyan Methodist Book Room, 1872).

quent ministry of John and Charles Wesley would mature into Methodism, which was itself a part of a larger evangelical revival.

This revival was marked by a period of renewal among many Anglo-American Protestant denominations that emphasized individual piety and devotion, born-again conversion experiences, and a rigorous faith-in-action. In the North American colonies, this movement was known as the First Great Awakening. As scholars have aptly shown, this renewal was a true transatlantic movement where sermons, tracts, and books were printed and reprinted across various English-speaking countries on either side of the Atlantic. The Wesleys and others (such as John's assistant, Francis Asbury) were vigorous itinerant preachers who gave themselves to intensive discipleship, small group accountability, and the care of fellow members. Methodism takes its name from these methods of disciplined living.

John Wesley had a desire to see Christians given practical tools to remain fervent in their prayer life, so he published several prayer books for public and private use. "Almighty and most merciful Father," an evening prayer that directed attention to God's sustaining work during the night, was published in one such book. This book cost two pence, roughly the price of a simple lunch, which covered printing and distribution among the destitute.

Source

94: John Wesley, *A Collection of Prayers for Families* (London: H. Cock, 1750), 7–8.

✎ 39. William Jay (1769–1853)

Christians today may be more familiar with William Jay's companions (such as Hannah More, William Wilberforce, and John Ryland) than Jay himself, but during his lifetime, Jay was a popular and influential preacher, and his skill in oration contributed to the respectability of evangelicalism among the British middle class. He served as an Independent minister at Argyle Chapel in Bath, England, for sixty-two years, beginning his tenure as an heir of the evangelical revival tradition in England.

Overall, he was concerned to see his hearers experience a genuine conversion and live a dedicated Christian life. Each of Jay's prayers within our volume comes from his prayer book, *The Domestic Minister's Assistant.* Jay was best known by his contemporaries for his preaching ability, and he wanted all Christians to be equipped to evangelize and make disciples. He believed that fathers were to be the primary spiritual leaders within their homes (i.e., the domestic minister) and published an entire collection of prayers that fathers could use to instruct and model piety within their household, thus carrying on the legacy of his evangelical tradition. "Oh Lord, help us remember" is a clipping from a Sunday morning family prayer reminding the reader that life's sorrows are ever-present but God's mercies are more. "God of all grace, Father of mercies" and "You are the author of all existence" turn attention to God as the source of life and the fulfillment of all human needs.

Source

95–97: William Jay, *Prayers for the Use of Families; Or, the Domestic Ministers' Assistant* (New York: Solomon King, 1824), 18, 24–26, 33–34.

40. Charles Spurgeon (1834–1892)

Perhaps no preacher is better known than Charles Haddon Spurgeon. He remains one of the most influential preachers in many Protestant denominations and his sermons, books, and tracts remain in print today, more than a century after his death.

Spurgeon was the pastor of New Park Street Chapel, which later became Metropolitan Tabernacle. This church already had a storied past before he joined—Reformed Baptists such as Benjamin Keach, John Rippon, and John Gill all pastored there in the prior centuries. Because of the throngs of people who came to hear Spurgeon preach, the New Park Street congregation was able to build the Metropolitan Tabernacle not long after Spurgeon's arrival in London. Overall, Spurgeon led a vigorous life—he established the Stockwell Orphanage and other charities, led the Pastors' College, edited the *Sword and Trowel* magazine, and championed the orthodox cause within the Baptist Union of Great Britain.

Like other evangelicals before him, Spurgeon enjoyed transatlantic recognition for his work. The publishing company started by D. L. Moody and Fleming H. Revell—which aimed at making works of practical devotion accessible for Christians everywhere—printed at least sixteen of Spurgeon's books as well as twenty-eight volumes of his sermons. Evangelicals loved reading Spurgeon's works, and that love has continued on today.

The two prayers "Oh you, who are King of kings and Lord of lords" and "Oh God, we would not speak to you from a distance" both feature extensive quotations from Scripture, which Spurgeon used to shape his prayers and claim God's promises. The second combined the themes of righteousness and justice using a line from a popular Isaac Watts hymn. Spurgeon was also comfortable weaving cultural references into his prayers. For instance, he quoted a line from the first stanza of William Cowper's "Timepiece," which is abolitionist in subject and tone. Spurgeon and Cowper both despised chattel slavery and implored the British Empire to do more to end it. Given the great popularity of Cowper's poem, Spurgeon knew his audience would make the connection to the issue of slavery. In sum, his prayer asks God for the help needed to advance the gospel and address the physical needs of neighbors. "Oh God, we would not speak to you from a distance" shows believers how to ask God to keep his promises on their account. In this prayer, Spurgeon relies heavily on Scriptural references as he focuses himself and his audience on the hard work of the kingdom set before them.

Source

98–99: C. H. Spurgeon, *Prayers from Metropolitan Pulpit: C. H. Spurgeon's Prayers* (New York: Fleming H. Revell, 1906), 9–14, 107–110.

Appendix

Original Language Texts

THE PRAYING COMMUNION of the church covers not only a long timeline but also a geographical and cultural breadth that reminds us of God's eternal covenant to bless all families of the earth and his corresponding promise that people from every tribe and language will worship him together. Our efforts to engage with representatives from a variety of those tribes and languages while still making the prayers of the community of saints accessible to our particular audience has required us to translate prayers originally written in a variety of languages other than English, including ancient and early modern ones, as well as early and modern English.

Yet, we also want to provide access to these prayers as they were first given to the church—in Greek, Latin, German, and earlier forms of English. The texts included in this appendix provide interested readers the opportunity to see these prayers in their original languages (with no editorial changes). The old adage is, after all, correct—something is always lost in translation, even in the best of translations. For those who find the original texts helpful, we are happy to offer them here, organized by corresponding prayer number. We hope that the entire collection, both in original language and in translation, will remind all readers of the diversity within the community of believers and draw them into a closer relationship with the one to whom these prayers are directed.

3. Prayer of Thanksgiving
The Didache (ca. 100) ❧ *1*

Ἐυχαριστοῦμέν σοι, πάτερ ἅγιε, ὑπὲρ τοῦ ἁγίου ὀνόματός σου, οὗ κατεσκήνωσας ἐν ταῖς καρδίαις ἡμῶν, καὶ ὑπὲρ τῆς γνώσεως καὶ πίστεως καὶ ἀθανασίας, ἧς ἐγνώρισας ἡμῖν διὰ Ἰησοῦ τοῦ παιδός σου· σοὶ ἡ δόξα εἰς τοὺς αἰῶνας.

σύ, δέσποτα παντοκράτωρ, ἔκτισας τὰ πάντα ἕνεκεν τοῦ ὀνόματός σου, τροφήν τε καὶ ποτὸν ἔδωκας τοῖς ἀνθρώποις εἰς ἀπόλαυσιν, ἵνα σοι εὐχαριστήσωσιν, ἡμῖν δὲ ἐχαρίσω πνευματικὴν τροφὴν καὶ ποτὸν καὶ ζωὴν αἰώνιον διὰ τοῦ παιδός σου.

Πρὸ πάντων εὐχαριστοῦμέν σοι, ὅτι δυνατὸς εἶ· σοὶ ἡ δόξα εἰς τοὺς αἰῶνας.

μνήσθητι, κύριε, τῆς ἐκκλησίας σου, τοῦ ῥύσασθαι αὐτὴν ἀπὸ παντὸς πονηροῦ καὶ τελειῶσαι αὐτὴν ἐν τῇ ἀγάπῃ σου, καὶ σύναξον αὐτὴν ἀπὸ τῶν τεσσάρων ἀνέμων, τὴν ἁγιασθεῖσαν, εἰς τὴν σὴν βασιλείαν, ἣν ἡτοίμασας αὐτῇ· ὅτι σού ἐστιν ἡ δύναμις καὶ ἡ δόξα εἰς τοὺς αἰῶνας.

ἐλθέτω χάρις καὶ παρελθέτω ὁ κόσμος οὗτος. Ὡσαννὰ τῷ υἱῷ Δαυείδ. εἴ τις ἅγιός ἐστιν, ἐρχέσθω· εἴ τις οὐκ ἔστι, μετανοείτω· μαρὰν ἀθά. ἀμήν.

4. Prayer of Hope for the Congregation
Clement of Rome (d. ca. 99) ❧ *2*

Δὸς ὑμῖν, Κύριε, ἐλπίζειν ἐπὶ τὸ ἀρχεγόνον πάσης κτίσεως ὄνομά σου, ἀνοίξας τοὺς ὀφθαλμοὺς τῆς καρδίας ἡμῶν εἰς τὸ γινώσκειν σε τὸν μόνον ὕψιστον ἐν ὑψίστοις, ἅγιον ἐν ἁγίοις ἀναπαυόμενον· τὸν ταπεινοῦντα ὕβριν ὑπερηφάνων, τὸν διαλύοντα λογισμοὺς ἐθνῶν, τὸν ποιοῦντα ταπεινοὺς εἰς ὕψος καὶ τοὺς ὑψηλοὺς ταπεινοῦντα, τὸν πλουτίζοντα καὶ πτωχίζοντα, τὸν ἀποκτείνοντα καὶ ζῆν ποιοῦντα, μόνον εὐεργέτην πνευμάτων καὶ θεὸν πάσης σαρκός· τὸν ἐπιβλέποντα ἐν τοῖς ἀβύσσοις, τὸν ἐπόπτην ἀνθρωπίνων ἔργων, τὸν τῶν κινδυνευόντων βοηθόν, τὸν τῶν ἀπηλπισμένων σωτῆρα, τὸν παντὸς πνεύματος κτίστην καὶ ἐπίσκοπον· τὸν πληθύνοντα ἔθνη ἐπὶ γῆς καὶ ἐκ πάντων ἐκλεξάμενον τοὺς ἀγαπῶντάς σε διὰ Ἰησοῦ

Χριστοῦ τοῦ ἠγαπημένου παιδός σου, δι' οὗ ἡμᾶς ἐπαίδευσας, ἡγίασας, ἐτίμησας.

ἀξιοῦμέν σε, δέσποτα, βοηθὸν γενέσθαι καὶ ἀντιλήπτορα ἡμῶν. τοὺς ἐν θλίψει ἡμῶν σῶσον, τοὺς ταπεινοὺς ἐλέησον, τοὺς πεπτωκότας ἔγειρον, τοῖς δεομένοις ἐπιφάνηθι, τοὺς ἀσθενεῖς ἴασαι, τοὺς πλανωμένους τοῦ λαοῦ σου ἐπίστρεψον· χόρτασον τοὺς πεινῶντας, λύτρωσαι τοὺς δεσμίους ἡμῶν, ἐξανάστησον τοὺς ἀσθενοῦντας, παρακάλεσον τοὺς ὀλιγοψυχοῦντας· γνώτωσάν σε ἅπαντα τὰ ἔθνη, ὅτι σὺ εἶ ὁ θεὸς μόνος καὶ Ἰησοῦς Χριστὸς ὁ παῖς σου καὶ ἡμεῖς λαός σου καὶ πρόβατα τῆς νομῆς σου.

Σὺ γὰρ τὴν ἀέναον τοῦ κόσμου σύστασιν διὰ τῶν ἐνεργουμένων ἐφανεροποίησας· σύ, κύριε, τὴν οἰκουμένην ἔκτισας, ὁ πιστὸς ἐν πάσαις ταῖς γενεαῖς, δίκαιος ἐν τοῖς κρίμασιν, θαυμαστὸς ἐν ἰσχύϊ καὶ μεγαλοπρεπείᾳ, ὁ σοφὸς ἐν τῷ κτίζειν καὶ συνετὸς ἐν τῷ τὰ γενόμενα ἑδράσαι, ὁ ἀγαθὸς ἐν τοῖς ὁρωμένοις καὶ χρηστὸς ἐν τοῖς πεποιθόσιν ἐπὶ σέ. ἐλεῆμον καὶ οἰκτίρμον, ἄφες ἡμῖν τὰς ἀνομίας ἡμῶν καὶ τὰς ἀδικίας καὶ τὰ παραπτώματα καὶ πλημμελείας.

μὴ λογίσῃ πᾶσαν ἁμαρτίαν δούλων σου καὶ παιδισκῶν, ἀλλὰ καθάρισον ἡμᾶς τὸν καθαρισμὸν τῆς σῆς ἀληθείας, καὶ κατεύθυνον τὰ διαβήματα ἡμῶν ἐν ὁσιότητι καρδίας πορεύεσθαι καὶ ποιεῖν τὰ καλὰ καὶ εὐάρεστα ἐνώπιόν σου καὶ ἐνώπιον τῶν ἀρχόντων ἡμῶν.

ναί, δέσποτα, ἐπίφανον τὸ πρόσωπόν σου ἐφ᾽ ἡμᾶς εἰς ἀγαθὰ ἐν εἰρήνῃ, εἰς τὸ σκεπασθῆναι ἡμᾶς τῇ χειρί σου τῇ κραταιᾷ καὶ ῥυσθῆναι ἀπὸ πάσης ἁμαρτίας τῷ βραχίονί σου τῷ ὑψηλῷ, καὶ ῥῦσαι ἡμᾶς ἀπὸ τῶν μισούντων ἡμᾶς ἀδίκως.

δὸς ὁμόνοιαν καὶ εἰρήνην ἡμῖν τε καὶ πᾶσιν τοῖς κατοικοῦσιν τὴν γῆν, καθὼς ἔδωκας τοῖς πατράσιν ἡμῶν, ἐπικαλουμένων σε αὐτῶν ὁσίως ἐν πίστει καὶ ἀληθείᾳ, ὑπηκόους γινομένους τῷ παντοκράτορι καὶ παναρέτῳ ὀνόματί σου, τοῖς τε ἄρχουσιν καὶ ἡγουμένοις ἡμῶν ἐπὶ τῆς γῆς.

Σύ, δέσποτα, ἔδωκας τὴν ἐξουσίαν τῆς βασιλείας αὐτοῖς διὰ τοῦ μεγαλοπρεποῦς καὶ ἀνεκδιηγήτου κράτους σου, εἰς τὸ γινώσκοντας ἡμᾶς τὴν ὑπὸ σοῦ αὐτοῖς δεδομένην δόξαν καὶ τιμὴν ὑποτάσσεσθαι αὐτοῖς, μηδὲν ἐναντιουμένους τῷ θελήματί σου· οἷς δός, κύριε, ὑγίειαν, εἰρήνην, ὁμόνοιαν, εὐστάθειαν, εἰς τὸ διέπειν αὐτοὺς τὴν ὑπὸ σοῦ δεδομένην αὐτοῖς ἡγεμονίαν ἀπροσκόπως.

σὺ γάρ, δέσποτα, ἐπουράνιε, βασιλεῦ τῶν αἰώνων, δίδως τοῖς υἱοῖς τῶν ἀνθρώπων δόξαν καὶ τιμὴν καὶ ἐξουσίαν τῶν ἐπὶ τῆς γῆς ὑπαρχόντων· σύ, κύριε, διεύθυνον τὴν βουλὴν αὐτῶν κατὰ τὸ καλὸν καὶ εὐάρεστον ἐνώπιόν σου, ὅπως διέποντες ἐν εἰρήνῃ καὶ πραΰτητι εὐσεβῶς τὴν ὑπὸ σοῦ αὐτοῖς δεδομένην ἐξουσίαν ἵλεώ σου τυγχάνωσιν.

ὁ μόνος δυνατὸς ποιῆσαι ταῦτα καὶ περισσότερα ἀγαθὰ μεθ᾽ ἡμῶν, σοὶ ἐξομολογούμεθα διὰ τοῦ ἀρχιερέως καὶ προστάτου τῶν ψυχῶν ἡμῶν Ἰησοῦ Χριστοῦ, δι᾽ οὗ σοι ἡ δόξα καὶ ἡ μεγαλωσύνη καὶ νῦν καὶ εἰς γενεὰν γενεῶν καὶ εἰς τοὺς αἰῶνας τῶν αἰώνων. Ἀμήν.

5. Prayer of Intercession
Polycarp (69–155) ❧ *3*

Deus autem et pater domini nostri Iesu Christi, et ipse sempi-
ternus pontifex, dei filius Iesus Christus, aedificet vos in fide
et veritate et in omni mansuetudine et sine iracundia et in
patientia et in longanimitate et tolerantia et castitate; et det
vobis sortem et partem inter sanctos suos et nobis vobiscum et
omnibus, qui sunt sub caelo, qui credituri sunt in dominum
nostrum et deum Iesum Christum et in ipsius patrem, qui
resuscitavit eum a mortuis.

7. Prayer for the Church
Hippolytus of Rome (ca. 170–ca. 235) ❧ *4*

Petimus ut mittas Spiritum tuum Sanctum in oblationem
sancta Ecclesiae. In unum congregans des omnibus qui percip-
iunt sanctis in repletionem Spiritus Sancti ad confirmationem
fidei in veritate, ut te laudemus et glorificemus per puerum
tuum Jesum Christum, per quem tibi gloria et honor Patri

et Filio cum Sancto Spiritu in sancta Ecclesia tua et nunc et
in saecula saeculorum. Amen.

8. Prayer before Receiving the Lord's Supper
Clementine Liturgy ✒ 5

Ὁ θεὸς ὁ μέγας καὶ μεγαλώνυμος, ὁ μέγας τῇ βουλῇ
καὶ κραταιὸς τοῖς ἔργοις, ὁ θεὸς καὶ Πατὴρ τοῦ ἁγίου
Παιδός σου Ἰησοῦ τοῦ Σωτῆρος ἡμῶν, ἐπίβλεψον ἐφ'
ἡμᾶς καὶ ἐπὶ τὸ ποίμνιόν σου τοῦτο, ὃ δι' αὐτοῦ ἐξελέξω
εἰς δόξαν τοῦ ὀνόματός σου, καὶ ἁγίασας ἡμῶν τὸ σῶμα
καὶ τὴν ψυχὴν καταξίωσον καθαροὺς γενομένους ἀπὸ
παντὸς μολυσμοῦ σαρκὸς καὶ πνεύματος, τυχεῖν τῶν
προκειμένων ἀγαθῶν, καὶ μηδένα ἡμῶν ἀνάξιον κρίνῃς,
ἀλλὰ βοηθὸς ἡμῶν γενοῦ, ἀντιλήπτωρ, ὑπερασπιστής,
διὰ τοῦ Χριστοῦ σου· μεθ' οὗ σοι δόξα, τιμή, αἶνος, δο-
ξολογία, εὐχαριστία, καὶ τῷ ἁγίῳ Πνεύματι, εἰς τοὺς
αἰῶνας. Ἀμήν.

9. Prayer for Enemies
Clementine Liturgy ✒ 5

Ἔτι παρακαλοῦμέν σε καὶ ὑπὲρ τῶν μισούντων ἡμᾶς καὶ
διωκόντων ἡμᾶς διὰ τὸ ὄνομά σου, ὑπὲρ τῶν ἔξω ὄντων
καὶ πεπλανημένων, ὅπως ἐπιστρέψῃς αὐτοὺς εἰς ἀγαθόν,
καὶ τὸν θυμὸν αὐτῶν πραΰνῃς.

10. Prayer for Divine Strength

The Clementine Liturgy ❧ 5

Oh Lord God Almighty—who hearest those who call upon thee with Uprightness—we give Thanks to thee, that thou hast vouchsafed to make us Partakers of thy holy Mysteries, which thou hast bestowed upon us, for the full Assurance of those Things which we rightly know, for our Preservation in Godliness, and for the Remission of our Sins; for the Name of thy Christ is called upon us, and we are joined unto Thee. Thou hast separated us from the Communion of the Ungodly, unite us with those that are sanctified unto Thee, establish us in the Truth by the Descent of thy holy Spirit, reveal to us what Things we are ignorant of, supply what we are deficient in; and strengthen us in what we know. Preserve the Priests unblameable in thy Service: keep the Kings in Peace, and the Rulers in Righteousness; the Air in good Temperature, the Fruits of the Earth in Plenty, and the whole World by thy all-powerful Providence. Pacify the Nations that delight in War; convert those that are in Error; sanctify thy People; preserve those that are in Virginity; keep those that are married in Fidelity; strengthen those who live in Chastity; bring the Infants to adult Age; confirm the newly initiated; instruct the Catechumens, and make them worthy of Initiation, and gather us all into thy Kingdom of Heaven, in Christ Jesus our Lord, with whom, to Thee be Glory, Honour, and Adoration, and to the Holy Ghost, World without end. Amen.

12. Prayer for Gifts from God

The Liturgy of Saint Chrysostom ❧ *7*

Almightie God, which haste geuen vs grace at this tyme with one accorde to make oure commune supplicacions vnto thee, and doest promise, that whan two or three be gathered in thy name, thou wylt graunte theyr requestes: fulfill nowe, O Lorde, the desyres and peticions of thy seruauntes, as may be moste expedience for them, grauntyng vs in this worlde knowlege of thy trueth, and in the worlde to come lyfe euerlastyng.

13. Prayer for the People of God

The Liturgy of Saint Chrysostom ❧ *7*

Μνήσθητι, Κύριε, τῆς πόλεως [ταύτης], ἐν ᾗ παροικοῦμεν καὶ πάσης πόλεως καὶ χώρας καὶ τῶν πίστει οἰκούντων ἐν αὐταῖς. Μνήσθητι, Κύριε, πλεόντων, ὁδοιπορούντων, νοσούντων, καμνόντων, αἰχμαλώτων καὶ τῆς σωτη-ρίας αὐτῶν. Μνήσθητι, Κύριε, τῶν καρποφορούντων καὶ καλλιεργούντων ἐν ταῖς ἁγίαις σου Ἐκκλησίαις καὶ μεμνημένων τῶν πενήτων, καὶ ἐπὶ πάντας ἡμᾶς τὰ ἐλέη σου ἐξαπόστειλον.

Καὶ δὸς ἡμῖν ἐν ἑνὶ στόματι καὶ μιᾷ καρδίᾳ δοξάζειν καὶ ἀνυμνεῖν τὸ πάντιμον καὶ μεγαλοπρεπὲς ὄνομά σου, τοῦ Πατρὸς καὶ τοῦ Υἱοῦ καὶ τοῦ Ἁγίου Πνεύματος, νῦν, καὶ ἀεί, καὶ εἰς τοὺς αἰῶνας τῶν αἰώνων.

17. Prayer for Protection
Old Gallican Rite ✤ *8*

Liberati a malo, confirmati semper in bono tibi servire mereamur Deo ac Domino nostro. Pone, Domine, finem peccatis nostris: da gaudium tribulatis, praebe redemptionem captivis, sanitatem infirmis, requiem defunctis: concede pacem et securitatem in omnibus diebus nostris. Frange audaciam inimicorum nostrorum et exaudi, Deus, orationes servorum tuorum omnium fidelium Christianorum in hac die et tempore. Per Dominum nostrum Iesum Christum Filium tuum, qui tecum vivit et regnat in unitate Spiritus Sancti Deus per omnia saecula saeculorum. Amen.

18. Prayer of Praise
Old Gallican Rite ✤ *5*

Dignum et justum est, aequum et justum est, te laudare, teque benedicere, tibi gratias agere, omnipotens sempiterne Deus.

Qui gloriaris in conventu Sanctorum tuorum, quos ante mundi constitutionem praeelectos spirituali in coelestibus benedictione signasti: quosque Unigenito tuo per adsumptionem carnis, et crucis redemptionem sociasti: in quibus Spiritum tuum Sanctum regnare fecisti, per quem ad felicis martyrii gloriam pietatis tuae favore venerunt.

19. Prayer of Thanksgiving for the Forgiveness of Sins
Old Gallican Rite ❧ *8*

Dignum et justum est, nos tibi gratias agere, Domine sancte, Pater omnipotens, aeterne Deus, per Jesum Christum Filium tuum Dominum nostrum, quem pro nobis omnibus tradi hostiam voluisti. O mira circa nos pietatis tuae dignatio! O ineffabilis dilectio caritatis; ut servum redimeres, Filium tradidisti! O certe necessarium Adae peccatum, quod Christe morte deletum est! O felix culpa, quae talem ac tantum meruit habere Redemptorem! Numquam enim quanta circa nos pietatis tuae dilectio esset, cognosceremus, nisi ex morte unici et coaeterni Filii tui Domini ac Dei nostri Jesu Christi probaremus. Vincit malitiam diaboli pietas tuae dignationis: quia ubi abundavit peccatum, superabundavit et gratia. Sed plus nobis tua misericordia reddidit, quam invidus inimicus abstulerat. Ille Paradisum invidit: tu coelos donasti. Ille mortem temporalem intulit; tu vitam perepetuam tribuisti.

Propterea profusis gaudiis totus in orbe terrarum mundus exultat: sed et supernae concinunt Potestates hymnum gloriae tuae, sine fine dicentes.

20. Prayer for Church Growth
Old Gallican Rite ❧ *8*

Vere dignum et justum est, unianimes et concordes omnipotentem Deum profusius deprecari cum unico Filio ejus Domino Jesu Christo Salvatore nostro, qui Ecclesiam suam secunda liberavit a morte, quando sanguis ipsius effusus est super cruce. Per ipsum te rogamus, omnipotens Deus: ut Ecclesiam tuam augeas in fide, custodias in spe, protegas in caritate: et sacrificia nostra libens suscipere digneris cum gloria et honore.

23. Prayer for a Pure Heart
Liturgy of Jerusalem and Saint James ❧ *9*

Καταξίωσον ἡμᾶς, δέσποτα φιλάνθρωπε, μετὰ παρρησίας, ἀκατακράτως, ἐν καθαρᾷ καρδίᾳ ἐπικαλεῖσθαί σε, τὸν ἐν τοῖς οὐρανοῖς ἅγιον θεόν, πατέρα, καὶ λέγειν.

24. Prayer for Sanctification
Liturgy of Jerusalem and Saint James ❧ *9*

O Lord Jesus Christ, the Son of the living God, the Lamb and the Shepherd who takest away the Sin of the World, who didst graciously remit to the two Debtors what they owed thee, and to the Woman who was a Sinner didst give the Pardon of her Sins, who with the Forgiveness of the Sins of the Paralytick didst grant him also a Cure of his Disease; remit, pardon, and forgive, O God, the Sins which [we] have committed willingly or unwillingly, with Knowledge or through Ignorance, by Transgression and Disobedience, which thy most holy Spirit knows thy Servants to have been guilty of; and wherein so ever, as Men clothed in Flesh, and Inhabitants of this World, or by *the Fraud of* the Devil they have been led astray from thy Commands in Word or Deed, or if they have become obnoxious to any Curse, or to any Imprecation upon themselves, I pray and beseech thee of thy ineffable Love to Man that they may be absolved by thy Word, and released from the Oath, and Imprecation upon themselves, according to thy great Goodness. Even so, O Lord, hear my Supplication for thy Servants, and as thou dost not delight in the Remembrance of Evil, over-look all their Offence, forgive all their Sins voluntary and involuntary and deliver them from eternal Punishment. For thou art he who hast enjoin'd us, saying, whatsoever ye shall loose on Earth shall be loosed in Heaven; thou art our God, a God who hast Power to have mercy, to save, and to forgive Sins; and to Thee, with thy unoriginate Father, and life-giving Spirit, belongs Glory, now and ever, World without end. Amen.

25. Prayer for Sanctification

Liturgy of Jerusalem and Saint James ❧ *9*

O good God, by the Grace of thy Christ, and the Descent of thy most holy Spirit; sanctify also, O Lord, our Souls, and Bodies, and Spirits, search our Minds, and examine our Consciences, and put away from us all evil Notions, all impure Thoughts, all filthy Lusts, all indecent Thoughts, all Envy, and Pride, and Hypocrisy, all Falshood, all Deceit, all worldly Solicitude, all Covetousness, all Vain-glory, all Sloth, all Malice, all Wrath, all Anger, all Remembrance of Injuries, all Evil speaking, and every Motion of Flesh and Spirit, that is contrary to the Will of thy Holiness.

26. Prayer for Blessing

Liturgy of Saint Mark ❧ *10*

We most earnestly beseech Thee, O Thou Lover of mankind, to bless all Thy people, the flocks of Thy fold. Send down into our hearts the peace of heaven, and grant us also the peace of this life. Give life to the souls of all of us, and let no deadly sin prevail against us, or any of Thy people. Deliver all who are in trouble, for Thou art our God, who settest the captives free; who givest hope to the hopeless, and help to the helpless; who liftest up the fallen; and who art the Haven of the shipwrecked.

Give Thy pity, pardon, and refreshment to every Christian soul, whether in affliction or error. Preserve us, in our pilgrimage through this life from hurt and danger, and grant that we may end our lives as Christians, well-pleasing to Thee and free from sin, and that we may have our portion and lot with all Thy saints. Amen.

27. Prayer for Illumination
Liturgy of Saint Mark ⇨ 10

O God of Light, Father of life, Author of grace, Creator of worlds, Founder of knowledge, Giver of wisdom, Treasure of holiness, Teacher of pure prayers, Benefactor of our souls, who givest to the faint-hearted who put their trust in Thee those things into which the angels desire to look: O Sovereign Lord, who hast brought us up from the depths of darkness to light, who hast given us life from death, who hast graciously bestowed upon us freedom from slavery, and who hast scattered the darkness of sin within us, through the presence of Thine only-begotten Son, do Thou now also, through the visitation of Thy all-holy Spirit, enlighten the eyes of our understanding and sanctify us wholly in soul, body, and spirit. [Amen.]

28. Prayer to Begin the Day
Liturgy of Saint Mark ❧ *10*

We give Thee thanks—yea, more than thanks O Lord our God, for all Thy goodness at all times, and in all places, because Thou hast shielded, rescued, helped, and guided us all the days of our lives, and brought us unto this hour. We pray and beseech Thee, merciful God, to grant in Thy goodness that we may spend this day, and all the time of our lives, without sin, in fullness of joy, holiness, and reverence of Thee. But drive away from us, O Lord, all envy, all fear, and all temptations.

Bestow upon us what is good and meet. Whatever sin we commit in thought, word, or deed, do Thou in Thy goodness and mercy be pleased to pardon. And lead us not into temptation, but deliver us from evil; through the grace, mercy, and love of Thine only begotten Son. Amen.

29. Prayer for Love
The Coptic Liturgy of Saint Cyril ❧ *11*

O God of love, Who hast given a new commandment through Thine only begotten Son, that we should love one another, even as Thou didst love us, the unworthy and the wandering, and gavest Thy beloved Son for our life and salvation; we pray Thee, Lord, give to us, Thy servants, in all time of our life on the earth, a mind forgetful of past ill-will, a pure conscience and sincere thoughts, and a heart to love our brethren; for the sake of Jesus Christ, Thy Son, our Lord and only Saviour. Amen.

35. Prayer for Heretics
Gregory of Nazianzus (329-390) ➤ *15*

ὁ δὲ ἀναγγέλλων συνδέσμους, καὶ λύων κρατούμενα, ὁ καὶ ἡμῖν ἐπὶ νοῦν ἀγαγὼν διαλῦσαι στραγγαλιὰς βιαίων δογμάτων, μάλιστα μὲν καὶ τούτους μεταβαλὼν ποιήσειεν πιστοὺς ἀντὶ τεχνολόγων, καὶ Χριστιανοὺς ἀνθ' ὧν νῦν ὀνομάζονται. τοῦτο δὴ καὶ παρακαλοῦμεν. δεόμεθα ὑπὲρ Χριστοῦ. καταλλάγητε τῷ θεῷ, καὶ τὸ πνεῦμα μὴ σβέννυτε. μᾶλλον δέ, καταλλαγείη Χριστὸς ὑμῖν, καὶ τὸ πνεῦμα ὀψὲ γοῦν ἀναλάμψειεν. εἰ δὲ λίαν ἔχοιτε φιλονείκως, ἀλλ᾽ ἡμεῖς γε σώζοιμεν ἡμῖν αὐτοῖς τὴν τριάδα, καὶ ὑπὸ τῆς τριάδος σωζοίμεθα, μένοντες εἰλικρινεῖς καὶ ἀπρόσκοποι, μέχρις ἀναδείξεως τελεωτέρας τῶν ποθουμένων, ἐν αὐτῷ Χριστῷ τῷ κυρίῳ ἡμῶν, ᾧ ἡ δόξα εἰς τοὺς αἰῶνας. Ἀμήν.

36. A Morning Prayer
Gregory of Nazianzus (329–390) ➤ *15*

'Tis dawn: to God I lift my hand,
To regulate my way;

My passions rule, and unmoved stand,
And give to Thee the day.
Not one dark word or deed of sin,
Not one base thought allow;
But watch all avenues within,
And wholly keep my vow.
Shamed were my age, should I decline;
Shamed were thy table too
At which I stand; thy will is mine;
Give grace, my Christ, to do.

39. Prayer for Knowledge of God
Augustine of Hippo (354-430) ❧ *17*

Magnus es, domine, et laudabilis valde. magna virtus tua et sapientiae tuae non est numerus. et laudare te vult homo, aliqua portio creaturae tuae, et homo circumferens mortalitatem suam, circumferens testimonium peccati sui et testimonium quia superbis resistis; et tamen laudare te vult homo, aliqua portio creaturae tuae. tu excitas ut laudare te delectet, quia fecisti nos ad te et inquietum est cor nostrum donec requiescat in te.

Da mihi, domine, scire et intellegere utrum sit prius invocare te an laudare te, et scire te prius sit an invocare te. sed quis te invocat nesciens te? aliud enim pro alio potest invocare nesciens. an potius invocaris ut sciaris? quomodo autem invocabunt, in quem non crediderunt? aut quomodo credent sine praedicante? et laudabunt dominum qui requirunt eum: quaerentes enim inveniunt eum et invenientes laudabunt eum. quaeram te, domine, invocans te et invocem te credens in te: praedicatus enim es nobis. invocat te, domine, fides mea, quam dedisti mihi, quam inspirasti mihi per humanitatem filii tui, per ministerium praedicatoris tui.

40. Prayer regarding God's Apparent Silence
Augustine of Hippo (354–430) ❧ *17*

Audeo dicere tacuisse te, deus meus, cum irem abs te longius? itane tu tacebas tunc mihi? et cuius erant nisi tua verba illa per matrem meam, fidelem tuam, quae cantasti in aures meas? . . . qui mihi monitus muliebres videbantur, quibus obtemperare erubescerem. illi autem tui erant et nesciebam, et te tacere putabam atque illam loqui per quam mihi tu non tacebas, et in illa contemnebaris a me, a me, filio eius, filio ancillae tuae, servo tuo.

41. Prayer for Mercy
Augustine of Hippo (354–430) ❧ *17*

Domine, miserere mei! ei mihi! ecce vulnera mea non abscondo. medicus es, aeger sum; misericors es, miser sum. numquid non temptatio est vita humana super terram? quis velit molestias et difficultates? tolerari iubes ea, non amari. nemo quod tolerat amat, etsi tolerare amat. quamvis enim gaudeat se tolerare, mavult tamen non esse quod toleret. prospera in adversis desidero, adversa in prosperis timeo. quis inter haec medius locus, ubi non sit humana vita temptatio? vae prosperitatibus saeculi semel et iterum a timore adversitatis et a corruptione laetitiae! vae adversitatibus saeculi semel et iterum et tertio a desiderio prosperitatis, et quia ipsa adversitas dura est, et ne frangat tolerantiam! numquid non temptatio est vita humana super terram sine ullo interstitio?

43. Prayer for Divine Approval
Augustine of Hippo (354–430) ✍ *17*

Cum ergo peruenerimus ad te, cessabunt multa ista quae dicimus et non peruenimus, et manebis unus omnia in omnibus, et sine fine dicemus unum laudantes te in unum et in te facti etiam nos unum. Domine deus une, deus trinitas, quaecumque dixi in his libris de tuo agnoscant et tui; si qua de meo, et tu ignosce et tui. Amen.

45. Prayer for Faith
Bede (673–735) ✍ *19*

Domine Deus noster, credimus in te Patrem, et Filium, et Spiritum sanctum. Neque enim diceret Veritas:

Ite, baptizate gentes in nomine Patris, et Filii, et Spiritus sancti, nisi Trinitas esses; nec baptizari nos juberes Domine Deus, in ejus nomine, qui non est Dominus Deus. Nec diceretur voce divina, *Audi Israel, Dominus Deus tuus Dominus unus est*, nisi Trinitas ita esses, ut unus Dominus Deus esses, et nisi tu Deus Pater ipse esses, et Filius Verbum tuum Jesus Christus ipse esses, et donum vestrum Spiritus sanctus, non legeremus in litteris Veritatis: *Misit Deus Filium suum*:

Nec tu Unigenite diceres de Spiritu sancto *quem mittit Pater in nomine meo, et quem ego mittam vobis a Patre*. Ad hanc regulam fidei dirigens intentionem meam, summa origo rerum, et perfectissima pulchritudo et beatissima delectatio.

46. Prayer for Protection
Bede (673–735) ❧ *19*

Liberator animarum, mundi Redemptor, Jesu Christe, Deus aeterne, rex immortalis, supplico ego peccator immensam clementiam tuam, ut per magnam misericordiam tuam, et per modulationem psalmorum, quam ego indignus peccator decantavi, liberes animam meam de peccato. Averte cor meum ab onmibus malis, pravis et perfidis cogitationibus, libera corpus meum de servitute peccati, repelle a me concupiscentiam carnalem, eripe me de omni impedimento satanae et ministrorum ejus visibilium et invisibilium, infidelium tuorum inimicorum quaerentium animam meam. Custodi me ab his et ab omnibus malis, Salvator mundi, qui cum Deo Patre et Spiritu-sancto vivis et regnas ac dominaris Deus per infinita saecula saeculorum. Amen.

47. Prayer in Praise of the Trinity
Bede (673–735) ❧ *19*

> Adesto mihi, una spes mea, Domine Deus meus.
> Adesto lumen verum, Pater omnipotens Deus.
> Adesto, lumen de Iumine et Verbum et Filius Dei, Deus
>   omnipotens.
> Adesto Sancte Spiritus, Patris et Filii concordia, Deus
>   omnipotens.
> Adesto, Deus unus omnipotens Pater et Filius et Spiritus
>   sanctus.
> Doce fidem, excita spem, infunde caritatem.
> Velle mihi adjacet, sed hoc non a me, sed a te,
> Mundum et terras linquere, et coelum petere,
> Sed imbecilla pluma est velle, sine subsidio tuo.
> Da fidei pennas ut volem sursum ad te.
> Hanc fidem in te, per te, de te confiteor.
> Te unum in substantia, Trinitatem in personis confiteor.
> Te semper idem esse, vivere, et intelligere confiteor.
> Et tres unum, et unum tres confiteor.

Pater et Filius et Spiritus sanctus. O beata Trinitas.

Deus, Dominus, Paracletus, O beata Trinitas.

Caritas, gratia, communicatio. O beata Trinitas.

Caritas Deus est, gratia Christus, communicatio Spiritus
sanctus. O beata Trinitas.

Genitor, Genitus, Regenerans. O beata Trinitas.

Verum lumen, verum ex lumine, vera illumninatio.
O beata Trinitas.

Invisibilis invisibiliter, Visibilis invisibiliter, Invisibilis
visibiliter. O beata Trinitas.

Fons, Flumen, Irrigatio. O beata Trinitas.

Ab Uno omnia, per Unum omnia, in Uno omnia.
O beata Trinitas.

A quo, per quem et in quo omnia. O beata Trinitas.

Vivens Vita, Vita a Vivente, Vivificator Viventium.
O beata Trinitas.

Unus a se, Unus ab Uno, Unus ab Ambobus. O beata
Trinitas.

Unus a se, Unus ab altero, Unus ab utroque. O beata
Trinitas.

Omne autem, Omne semper in tribus, et omne Omne
aequaliter in singulis. O beata Trinitas.

Verus Pater, veritas Filius, veritas Spiritus sanctus.
O beata Trinitas.

Una igitur Pater, ΛΟΓΟΣ, Paracletusque substantia est.
O beata Trinitas.

Una essentia, una virtus, una bonitas omnia. O beata
Trinitas.

Deus beatitudo, in quo et a quo et per quem beata sunt
quaecumque beata sunt. O beata Trinitas.

Deus vera et summa vita, in quo et a quo et per quem
vivunt quaecunque vere summeque vivunt omnia.
O beata Trinitas.

Deus bonum et pulchrum, in quo et a quo et per quem
bona et pulcra sunt quaecunque bona et pulcra
sunt omnia. O beata Trinitas.

Deus cui nos fides excitat, spes erigit, caritas jungit.
O beata Trinitas.

Deus qui petere jubes et invenire facis, et pulsantibus
aperis. O beata Trinitas.

Deus supra quem nihil, extra quem nihil, sine quo nihil.
O beata Trinitas.

Deus sub quo totum, in quo totum, cum quo totum.
O beata Trinitas.

Te invocamus, te adoramus, te laudamus. O beata
Trinitas.

Exaudi, exaudi, exaudi, o beata Trinitas.

Spes nostra, salus nostra, honor noster. O beata
    Trinitas.
Auge in nobis fidem, auge spem, auge caritatem.
    O beata Trinitas.
Libera nos, salva nos, justifica nos. O beata Trinitas.
Miserere, Domine, quia misericordia tua liberavit nos.
    O beata Trinitas.
Miserere, Domine, quia misericordia tua credimus in te.
    O beata Trinitas.
Miserere, Domine, quia misericordia tua credimus te.
    O beata Trinitas.
Miserere, Domine, quia misericordia tua speramus in te.
    O beata Trinitas.
Miserere, Domine, quia misericordia tua amamus te.
    O beata Trinitas.
Te adoramus cuncti unum Deum Patrem et Filium,
    Sanctumque Spiritum. O beata Trinitas.
Da peccatis veniam, praesta aeternam vitam, dona
    pacem et gloriam. O beata Trinitas.
O beata et benedicta et gloriosa Trinitas, Pater et Filius
    et Spiritus sanctus. O beata Trinitas.
O beata, benedicta, gloriosa Unitas Pater, Filius, et
    Spiritus sanctus. O beata Trinitas.

O vera, summa, sempiterna Trinitas Pater, et Filius, et
Spiritus sanctus. O beata Trinitas.
O vera, summa, sempiterna Unitas, Pater, et Filius, et
Spiritus sanctus. O beata Trinitas.
Miserere nobis, miserere nobis, miserere nobis. O beata
Trinitas. Tibi laus, tibi gloria, tibi gratiarum actio
in saecula sempiterna. Amen.

48. Prayer for the Conversion of One's Father
John of Damascus (ca. 675–749) ❧ *20*

ἴδε μου, Δέσποτα, τὴν συντριβὴν τῆς καρδίας ἵλεῳ
καὶ εὐμενεῖ ὄμματι· καὶ κατὰ τὴν ἀψευδῆ σου ἐπαγ-
γελίαν γενοῦ μετ' ἐμοῦ τοῦ γινώσκοντος καὶ ὁμολο-
γοῦντός σε ποιητὴν καὶ προνοητὴν πάσης κτίσεως.
πηγασάτω ἐν ἐμοὶ τὸ σὸν ἀλλόμενον ὕδωρ· καὶ δοθήτω
μοι λόγος ἐν ἀνοίξει τοῦ στόματος, καὶ νοῦς καλῶς
ἡδρασμένος ἐν σοὶ τῷ ἀκρογωνιαίῳ λίθῳ, ἵνα δυνή-
σομαι ὁ ἀχρεῖος οἰκέτης σου καταγγεῖλαι τῷ ἐμῷ γεν-
νήτορι, ὡς δεῖ, τὸ μυστήριον τῆς σῆς οἰκονομίας, καὶ
ἀποστῆσαι αὐτὸν τῇ σῇ δυνάμει τῆς ματαίας πλάνης
τῶν πονηρῶν δαιμόνων, καὶ προσαγαγεῖν σοι τῷ Θεῷ
καὶ δεσπότῃ, τῷ μὴ βουλομένῳ τὸν θάνατον ἡμῶν τῶν
ἁμαρτωλῶν, ἀλλ' ἀναμένοντι τὴν ἐπιστροφὴν καὶ τὴν
μετάνοιαν, ὅτι δεδοξασμένος εἶ εἰς τοὺς αἰῶνας. ἀμήν.

50. Prayer for Devotion to God
Anselm (1033/34–1109) ✍ *21*

Oro, Deus, cognoscam te, amem te, ut gaudeam de te. Et si non possum in hac vita ad plenum, vel proficiam in dies, usque dum veniat illud ad plenum. Proficiat hic in me notitia tui et ibi fiat plena; crescat amor tuus et ibi sit plenus, ut hic gaudium meum sit in spe magnum, et ibi sit in re plenum. Domine, per Filium tuum iubes, immo consulis petere et promittis accipere, "ut gaudium nostrum plenum sit" [Joh 16,24]. Peto, Domine, quod consulis "per admirabilem consiliarium" [Jes 9,6] nostrum; accipiam, quod promittis per veritatem tuam, "ut gaudium meum plenum sit" [Joh 16,24]. Deus verax, peto accipiam, "ut gaudium meum plenum sit" [Joh 16,24]. Meditetur interim inde mens mea, loquatur inde lingua mea. Amet illud cor meum, sermonicetur os meum. Esuriat illud omnia mea, sitiat caro mea, desideret tota substantia mea, donec "intrem in gaudium Domini mei" [Mt 25,21], qui est trinus et unus Deus "benedictus in saecula. Amen" [Rom 1,25].

51. Prayer to Strengthen Love for God
Anselm (1033/34–1109) ✍ *21*

Domine Jesu Christe, redemptio mea, misericordia mea, salus mea, te laudo, tibi gratias ago, quamvis valde impares tuis beneficiis, quamvis multum expertes dignae devotionis, quamvis nimis macras a desiderata pinguedine dulcissimi tui affectus: tamen qualescumque laudes, qualescumque gratias, non quales scio me debere; sed sicut potest conari, tibi persolvit anima mea.

Spes cordis mei, virtus animae meae, auxilium infirmitatis meae, compleat tua potentissima benignitas, quod conatur mea tepidissima imbecillitas. Vita mea, finis intentionis meae, etsi nondum merui tetantum, quantum debitor sum, amare; utique saltem desidero te tantum amare, quantum debeo.

52. Prayer of Longing for God
Anselm (1033/34–1109) ❧ *21*

Obsecro, Domine, amaricatum est cor meum sua desolatione, indulca illud tua consolatione. Obsecro, Domine, esuriens incepi quaerere te, ne desinam ieiunus de te. Famelicus accessi, ne recedam impastus. Pauper veni ad divitem, miser ad misericordem, ne redeam vacuus et contemptus. Et si"antequam comedam, suspiro" [Iob 3,24], da vel post suspiria quod comedam. Domine, incurvatus non possum nisi deorsum aspicere; erige me, ut possim sursum intendere. "Iniquitates meae supergressae caput meum" obvolvunt me, "et sicut onus grave" [Ps 37,5] gravant me. Evolve me, exonera me, ne "urgeat puteus" earum "os suum super me" [Ps 68,16]. Liceat mihi suspicere lucem tuam, vel de longe, vel de profundo. Doce me quaerere te et ostende te quaerenti; quia nec quaerere te possum, nisi tu doceas, nec invenire, nisi te ostendas. Quaeram te desiderando, desiderem quaerendo. Inveniam amando, amem inveniendo.

53. Prayer to the Holy Spirit
Anselm (1033/34–1109) ❧ *21*

Veni jam, veni, benignissime dolentis animae consolator in opportunitatibus, & in tribulationibus adjutor. Veni mundator scelerum, curator vulnerum. Veni fortitudo fragilium, relevator labentium, veni humilium doctor, superborum destructor. Veni ophanorum pius pater, viduarum dulcis Judex. Veni spes pauperum, refocillator deficentium. Veni navigantium sydus, naufragantium portus. Veni omnium viventium singulare decus, morientium unica salus. Veni sanctissime Spiritus, veni, & miserere mei, apta me tibi: & condescende propitius mihi, ut mea tuae magnitudini exiguitas, roborique tuo mea imbecillitas, secundum multitudinem tuarum complaceat miserationum, per Jesum Christum Salvatorem meum, qui cum Patre in tua unitate vivit & regnat in saecula saeculorum. Amen.

54. Prayer for Forgiveness
Anselm (1033/34–1109) ❧ *21*

Immensam misericordiam tuam, misericors Deus & miserator, iterum exoro, remitte mihi omnes lubricae temeritatis offensas; ut anima mea benignitatis tuae dulcedine repleatur, & concessa venia plenae indulgentiae, quidquid pro proprio reatu delibui, totum per ineffabilem pietatem tuam dele & absterge. Nec sit a me clementiae tuae longinqua miseratio; sed quidquid tuae voluntati contrarium, fallente diabolo, & propria iniquitate atque fragilitate contraxi, tu pius & misericors ablue indulgendo. Sana vulnera, cunctaque remitte peccata; ut nullis a te iniquitatibus separatus, sed semper hic & ubique defensionis tuae auxilio munitus, tibi Domino semper valeam adhaere, & perpetuae gloriae quandoque portionem percipere, quam oculus non vidit, & auris non audivit, & in cor hominis non ascendit, quae praeparasti diligentibus te. Amen.

55. Prayer for God to Hear My Prayer
Anselm (1033/34–1109) ❧ *21*

Exaudi me, exaudi, magne Domine, & bone Domine, cujus amoris affectu sese pascere desiderat, sed satiare se de te non potest famelica anima mea: ad quem invocandum non invenit os meum nomen, quod sufficiat cordi meo. Nullum enim verbum hoc mihi sapit, quod te donante affectus meus de te capit. Oravi, Domine, ut potui; sed plus volui, quam potui.

Exaudi, exaudi tu, sicuit potes, qui quod vis potes. Oravi ut infirmus & peccator; exaudi, exaudi tu, sicut potens &

miserator: & non solum amicis & inimicis meis, quae precatus sum, tribuas; sed sicut scis unicuique expedire, & voluntati tuae non disconvenire, omnibus vivis & defunctis misercordiae tuae remediae distribuas: & me non sicut vult cor meum, nec sicut petit os meum; sed sicut scis & vis me debere velle & petere, semper exaudias, Salvator mundi, qui cum Patre & Spiritu sancto vivis & regnas Deus per omnia saecula saeculorum. Amen.

56. Prayer for God to Act in Mercy
Anselm (1033/34–1109) ❧ *21*

I know, O Lord God, Thou Ruler of my life, that every best gift and every perfect gift is from above, coming down from the Father and Fountain of lights (St. James i. 16). I know that I can offer no acceptable pleasing thing to Thee, unless I have first drawn it from the Fountain of Thy goodness: and this only if Thou enlighten and if Thou teach me. I know that this earnest of Thy mercy must go before all effort of mine. I know, dearest Father, that if I cannot pilfer or filch away Thy good things from Thee, equally impossible is it for me, by any merits of mine, to procure the means where by to return to Thee and please Thee. For what due can merits of mine procure me but the punishment of eternal death? I know that it rests with Thy good pleasure whether Thou destroy me, according to the multitude of my evil deeds, my offences, my neglects, and my omissions; or remake me, and make me acceptable to Thee after the inestimable riches of Thy mercy; for Thou, the sole maker of Thy creature, canst alone re-make it.

57. Prayer to Know Christ

Bonaventure (1221–1274) ❧ *22, quoting Anselm*

Nondum ergo, Domine, dixi aut cogitavi, quantum gaudebunt illi beati tui. Utique tantum gaudebunt, quantum amabunt; tantum amabunt, quantum congoscent. Quantum cognoscent te et quantum amabunt te? Certe nec oculus vidit, nec auris audivit, nec in cor hominis ascendit in hac vita, quantum te congoscent et amabunt in illa vita.

Oro, Deus, cognoscam te, amen te, ut gaudeam de te; et si non possum ad plenum in hac vita, vel proficiam in dies, usque dum veniat illud ad plenum; proficiat hic in me notitia tui et ibi fiat plena; crescat hic amor tuus et ibi sit plenus; ut hic gaudium meum sit in spe magnum et ibi sit in re plenum.

Domine per Filium tuum iubes, immo consulis petere, et promittis accipere, ut gaudium nostrum plenum sit. Deus verax, peto, accipiam, ut gaudium meum plenum sit. Peto, Domine, quod per admirabilem consiliarium nostrum con-

sulis: accipiam, quod promittis per veritatem tuam ut gaudium meum plenum sit.

Meditetur interim inde mens mea loquatur inde lingua
mea, amet illud cor meum, sermocinetur os meum, esuriat
illud anima mea, sitiat caro mea, desideret tota substantia
mea, donec intrem in gaudium Domini mei, qui est trinus et
unus Deus benedictus in saecula saeculorum. Amen.

58. Prayer for Understanding God
Bonaventure (ca. 1221–1274) ✎ *22*

Let Us devoutly bow the knees of our heart, before the Throne
of the Eternall Majesty, and with teares and groans before
the Royall seate of the Judiciall Trinity, let Us incessantly
pray, that God the Father, by his blessed Sonne, would grant
us, the grace of mentall Exercise in the Holy Ghost, that we
may know, what is the breadth and length, and depth, and
height, that by this we may attaine to that which is the end
and complement of of [sic] all our desires. Amen.

59. Prayer for Right Desires
Thomas Aquinas (1225–1274) ✎ *23*

Concede mihi, misericors Deus, quae tibi sunt placita, ar-
denter concupiscere, prudenter investigare, veraciter agnos-
cere, et perfecte adimplere ad laudem et gloriam Nominis tui.

Ordina, Deus meus, statum meum et quod a me requiris, ut faciam, tribue ut sciam; et da exsequi sicut oportet et expedit animae meae.

Da mihi, Domine Deus meus, inter prospera et adversa non deficere, ut in illis non extollar, et in istis non deprimar. De nullo gaudeam vel doleam, nisi quod ducat ad te, vel abducat a te. Nulli placere appetam, vel displicere timeam nisi tibi.

Vilescant mihi, Domine, omnia transitoria, et cara mihi sint omnia aeterna. Taedeat me gaudii quod est sine te, nec aliud cupiam quod extra te. Delectet me, Domine, labor, qui est pro te; et taediosa sit mihi omnis quies, quae est sine te.

Da mihi, Deus meus, cor meum ad te dirigere, et in defectione mea cum emendationis proposito constanter dolere.

Fac me, Domine Deus meus, oboedientem sine contradictione, pauperem sine deiectione, castum sine corruptione, patientem sine murmuratione, humilem sine fictione, hilarem sine dissolutione, maturum sine gravedine, agilem sine levitate, timentem te sine desperatione, veracem sine duplicitate, operantem bona sine praesumptione, proximum corripere sine elatione, ipsum aedificare verbo et exemplo sine simulatione.

Da mihi, Domine Deus, cor pervigil, quod nulla abducat a te curiosa cogitatio: da nobile, quod nulla deorsum trahat indigna affectio; da rectum, quod nulla seorsum obliquet sinistra intentio: da firmum, quod nulla frangat tribulatio: da liberum, quod nulla sibi vindicet violenta affectio.

Largire mihi, Domine Deus meus, intellectum te cognoscentem, diligentiam te quaerentem, sapientiam te invenientem, conversationem tibi placentem, perseverantiam fidenter te expectantem, et fiduciam te finaliter amplectentem. Da tuis poenis hic affligi per paenitentiam, tuis beneficiis in via uti per gratiam, tuis gaudiis in patria perfrui per gloriam: Qui vivis et regnas Deus per omnia saecula saeculorum. Amen.

60. Prayer for Students
Thomas Aquinas (1225–1274) ✎ *23*

Creator ineffabilis, qui de thesauris sapientiae tuae tres Angelorum hierarchias designasti et eas super caelum empyreum miro ordine collocasti atque universi partes elegantissime distribuisti: Tu, inquam, qui verus fons luminis et sapientiae diceris ac supereminens principium, infundere digneris super intellectus mei tenebras tuae radium claritatis, duplices, in quibus natus sum, a me removens tenebras, peccatum scilicet et ignorantiam. Tu, qui linguas infantium facis disertas, linguam meam erudias atque in labiis meis gratiam tuae benedictionis infundas. Da mihi intelligendi acumen, retinendi capacitatem, addiscendi modum et facilitatem, interpretandi subtilitatem, loquendi gratiam copiosam. Ingressum instruas, progressum dirigas, egressum compleas. Tu, qui es verus Deus et homo, qui vivis et regnas in saecula saeculorum. Amen.

61. Prayer of Thanksgiving for God's Blessing
Thomas Aquinas (1225–1274) ✽ *23*

Laudo, glorifico, benedico te, Deus meus, propter immensa indigno mihi praestita beneficia.

Laudo clementiam tuam me diu expectantem, dulcedinem tuam ulcisci simulantem, pietatem tuam vocantem, benignitatem suscipientem, misericordiam peccata remittentem, bonitatem supra merita impendentem, patientiam injuriae non recordantem, humilitatem consolantem, patientiam protegentem, aeternitatem conservantem, veritatem remunerantem.

Quid dicam, Deus meus, de tua ineffabili largitate?

Tu enim vocas fugientem. Suscipis revertentem. Adjuvas titubantem. Laetificas desperantem. Stimulas negligentem. Armas pugnantem. Coronas triumphantem. Peccatorem post poenitentiam non spernis. Et injuriae non memineris, a multis liberas periculis. Ad poenitentiam cor emollis. Terres suppliciis. Allicis promissis. Castigas flagellis. Angelico ministerio custodis.

Ministras temporalia. Reservas nobis aeterna. Hortaris dignitate creationis. Invitas clementia redemptionis. Promittis praemia remunerationis.

Pro quibus omnibus laudes referre non sufficio.

Majestati tuae gratias ago propter immensae bonitatis tuae abundantiam, ut semper in me gratiam multiplices, et multiplicatam conserves, et conservatam remuneres. Amen.

62. Prayer for Receiving God
Thomas Bradwardine (ca. 1290–1349) ✽ *24*

My God, I love thee for thyself above all other things. I long for thee thyself. I desire thee as my final aim. Thyself for thyself, and no other thing, I seek always and in all things, with all my heart and veins, with crying and groaning, with continual labour and grief. What then wilt thou finally render me? if not thyself thou renderest nothing. If thou givest me not thyself thou givest nothing. If I find thee not I find nothing, By no means dost thou reward me, but heavily afflict me; for before I sought thee I hoped at length to find and retain thee, and by this delightful hope I was sweetly comforted in all my labours. But now, if thou shalt deny me thyself, whatever else thou mayest give, being disappointed of such a hope, not for a short time but for ever, shall I not always languish with desire, mourn with languishing, sorrow with mourning, wail and weep with sorrow, because I shall ever remain empty and unsatisfied. Shall I not grieve inconsolably, complain unceasingly, be vexed interminably? This is not thy way, O best, most gracious, most loving God. It agrees not with thee, it befits not thee. Grant, therefore, O my most blessed God, that in the present life I may ever love thee for thyself above all things, seek thee in all things, and at length, in the life to come, find and possess thee for ever.

63. Prayer of the Humble Servant
Thomas à Kempis (1380–1471) ❧ 25

O Most sweet, and loving Lord, whom I now desire to receive with all devotion, thou knowest my infirmity and the necessity which I endure, with how many sins and evils I am oppressed, how often I am grieved, tempted, troubled, and defiled. I come unto thee for remedy, I crave of thee comfort and succor; I speak to him that knoweth all things, to whom all my inward parts are open, and who can only perfectly comfort and help me. Thou knowest what good things I stand in most need of, and how poor I am in vertues.

Behold, I stand before thee poor and naked, calling for grace, and craving mercy. Refresh thy hungry beggar, inflame my coldness with the fire of thy love; inlighten my blindness with the brightness of thy presence. Turn all earthly things to me into bitterness, all things grievous and cross into patience, all low and created things into contempt and oblivion. Lift up my heart to thee in Heaven, and suffer me not to wander upon Earth. Be thou only sweet unto me from henceforth for evermore; for thou only art my meat and my drink, my love and my joy, my sweetness and all my good.

O that with thy presence thou wouldest wholly inflame, burn and conform me unto thy self; that I might be made one spirit with thee by the grace of inward union, and by the meltings of ardent love! Suffer me not to go from thee hungry and dry, but deal mercifully with me, as thou hast oftentimes dealt wonderfully with thy Saints. What marvel is it if I should be wholly inflamed by thee, and die from my self, sith thou art fire always burning and never decaying, love purifying the heart, and enlightning the understanding?

64. Prayer for Hope

Thomas à Kempis (1380–1471) ✎ *25*

Thine eies did see mee, when I was without forme.

O Lord my GOD, what in the ende will become of mee, seeing dailie I doo offend?

When shall I amend my life as I ought to doo? When will it be better with mee? When shall I waxe strong? And when shall I ouercome?

I am cast head-long into the deep pit of filthines. Who can thinke there is yet hope left to arise againe, to amend, to goe forward, and to come vnto the ende? Surelie touching my selfe I am out of all hope; ah that mine hope were stronger in thee!

I greatlie doo despeire, because my weakenes encreaseth through long troubles; and I see no ende of my sorow, and sinne.

And though I saie, lo nowe I will begin to amend; lo it is nowe time, I will doo my best to reforme my selfe, straight-waie, alas, sinne standeth before mee, the enimie lifteth vp himselfe against mee, and wicked custome keepeth mee back with might and maine, contrarie to my minde.

O Lord, behold howe I am cast downe, and troden vnder foote: behold the troubles which I doo endure.

Lift vp thy right hand, and deliuer mee fro my persecutors, for they are too strong for mee.

My wisedome is perished, and my strength hath failed mee.

Mine arme is broken, neither can my swoord saue mee.

I see not vnto whome I may flie; and that will receaue and heale me, I knowe none.

Thou alone continuest my refuge, but I dare not approch for shame, because I haue offended thee.

I haue sinned, ô God, forgiue mee. I am sorie, yea hartelie sorie that euer I did transgresse thy lawes.

Giue mee that which seemeth right in thine eies, and bee mercifull.

Thou didest iustlie in forsaking mee, and iustlie thou didest commit mee into the hands of mine aduersarie.

But Lord, remember that which thou hast made, amende that which is decaied, for of it selfe it can neuer stande.

Marke my groaning, and my troubles: let the paine and griefe of mine heart at no time be out of thy remembrance.

O mercifull Father, cast an eie vpon my thraldome and imprisonment, vpon the miserie and crueltie which I doo endure; and bring mee out that am bound, from the prison-house, and wretched bondage.

Though a man should liue manie yeares, what will hee bee the better thereby? And who knoweth whether hee shall amend his wicked life, or be worse and worse?

Man woteth not howe hee shall proceede, and ende; and his continuance is verie doubtfull, because of the manifold chances of euils, and dangerous tentations.

Manie at their first conuersion from sinne are good and humble, which afterward become froward and rebellious. At the first they were modest and deuoute, zelous and silent, and in the ende prooued carelesse, and dissolute, bablers, and barbarous. And they which at the beginning did bridle their wicked affections, at the length had scarse anie care at all either what they said or did. And so by little and little wickednesse taketh roote and encreaseth while it is not preuented at the beginning.

Who therefore but should feare, and be circumspect, seeing such vnluckie chances doo come vnto the good and modest?

Againe, who thoroughlie doth knowe whether hee bee elected; or hath strength to beare all things?

Wee are all to be tried, and who is sure that hee shall not be burned, seeing tentation is a fire?

So that all must feare, and hope alike of the better: but none is rashlie to presume, nor yet prowdlie to bee secure.

In deed the gold which is tried, shall be preserued: but I aduise thee, ô man, to consider well of what metall thou art.

The celestiall purger will purge, hee will fine the sonnes of Leui, euen all that are his seruants.

It is not alwaies gold, which hath the color of gold; neither is it alwaie stuble, or naughtie siluer, which endureth beating, and beareth the flaile. For God beholdeth the verie cogitations and the hearts, by them most commonlie working woonders, which in the opinion of manie are but castawaies.

O Lord God, what ioie can I haue in this world, when I thinke vpon the vncertaintie, and frailtie of all things vnder heauen?

Notwithstanding, this am I sure of, that thou art good, and that thy mercie is from generation to generation on them that feare thee.

For thine infinite goodnes and mercie, is greater than all my sins. And this shall be my comfort, while thou giuest me space to amend my life.

65. Prayer regarding the Miseries of This Life
Thomas à Kempis (1380–1471) ❧ *25*

Let mee vnderstand the shortnes of my daies. So long as I am in this world, I am wicked: and while I continue vpon the earth, I am poore, a stranger, and a pilgrime.

I brought nothing into the world, and certaine it is I can carrie nothing thereout: for naked came I out of my mothers wombe, and naked shall I returne thether againe.

As a shadow which passeth awaie; and as a fether, which is tossed vp and downe with the winde; and as a ghest of one night, so suddenlie shall I passe awaie.

All the time wee haue heere to liue, is but as the shortest night. Fewe and euill are my daies, and after a little while they shall ende, and bee as though they had neuer been.

And when man is dead, what is in man but filthines? Who will haue anie care of a stinking carkas? Or who will enquire of the absent being dead, whereas beeing aliue hee was accounted of?

A small while is man remembred either of his freends, or of strangers: but vndoubtedlie the righteous shall be had in euerlasting remembrance, because hee shall be euerlast-inglie linkèd to God, who is alwaies the same, and shall neuer die.

Therefore happie is hee which putteth no trust in man; nor yet reioiceth in anie worldlie thing, but hath his hart fixed in heauen, for what soeuer is in this world, is transitorie and vane.

Call into thy minde those which haue liued since the world began vntill nowe, and tell, I praie thee, where they bee? And those whome you see and heare to liue now, how long thinkest thou will they endure?

Saie therefore of all, Euerie man that liueth, is but vanitie.

O miserable and wretched life! ô fraile, and lamentable life, which good men doo suffer rather than desire: and wicked men, albe they desire it, yet can they not long enioie the same!

Oah, vanitie of this world, when wilt thou haue an ende? when wilt thou cesse?

Yet the time will come, when all the elect shall be set free from the bondage of corruption, though now they doo lament, because they are estranged from the kingdome of Christ.

Would to God, the whole world would euen wither vp in mine hart; and my Lord God, euen mine immortall spouse, seeme sweete vnto my soule!

Vndoubtedlie, the fleeting ioie of this present life, is but a false and a most bitter potion. Let them drinke thereof that list, for afterward they shall feele a most bitter flixe. And the more one hath drunke thereof, the sharper shall his torments bee, because the whole pleasure of this world shall more spee-delie passe awaie than the winde, and leaue to their louers paines and burnings.

Therefore out of my sight thou deceiptfull glorie of the world, and all foolish pleasure of the flesh.

Manie you doo drawe, and deceiue: but in the ende you leaue and destroie them.

Woe to them which beleeue thee; woe to them which be there drowned.

But come, and come nigh mee, most holie humilitie; and the full renouncing of all worldlie pompes; and neuer doo thou leaue mee, ô thou sweete remembrance of my present pilgrimage.

What am I but ashes, and earth? and whether tende I, but towardes earth?

Oah, how wretched am I become! how iustlie maie I la-ment, when I thinke vpon my pilgrimage, and how little I am priuie how I shall ende the same!

If I liue well, and continue so, there is no cause whie I should feare an euill death. But who can glorie of a good life, and of a pure conscience? Hee which knoweth himselfe to be such a one, let him reioice in the Lord, and take compassion vpon mee a sinner.

To liue I haue no desire, because miserie enuironeth mee on euerie side: to die an euill conscience is affraide, for to answeare God, it hath not one for a thousand.

The Prophet was not so in a feare, which said, *Mine heart is prepared, ô God,* mine heart is prepared.

O Lord, the God of my saluation, let my life come vnto a good ende; and prolong not the daies of my lamentation. With sorowe I came into this prison; and without griefe I shall not get out. . . .

Long doo I thinke this life; and the rather, because of the continuall miserie and troubles which I finde therein: but in truth it is not long, for it passeth awaie more swiftlie than a Poste.

To a man that liueth in paine and miserie, all time is long, and hee compteth a daie for a yeere. This maketh my life tedious vnto mee, and so much the more it dooth trouble mee, as the more trulie I consider all the miseries of the same.

But, if happelie anie consolations and ioie come between, it standeth mee vpon to looke about whether they bee of God, or no. If they be of God, I accept them gladlie, but yet

I knowe not how long they will continue: yet howe shorte soeuer they bee, they like and please mee well.

But, would to God hee would powre them largelie vpon mee; and cause them to continue with mee a long while!

But the ioies and pleasures which are not of God, are vile and vading, albe to the showe they appeare sweete and pleasant.

Thus, euen thus passeth awaie this life, replenished continuallie both with good and euill things.

Therefore so long as I liue in this world, I am a poore pilgrime.

I cannot trulie saie I haue enough, because presentlie there is saietie of no good thing: but the good thing which I looke for thou art, in whome I beleeue.

So that, when thy glorie hath appeared, and replenished mee, then, euen then I will acknowledge, that I haue enough. But in the meane while, because this word is hidden fro mee, much griefe and sorowe dooth enuiron my soule.

And therefore beeing mindfull of thine holie saieng, I repeate this often-times, *My soule is verie heauie, euen vnto the death.*

Well were it with mee, if this houre were come, and that neither griefe nor sorowe did possesse mee!

But, Lord, I beseech thee, let thy goodnes conserue mee.

66. Prayer to be Filled by God
Martin Luther (1483–1546) ❧ *26*

Sihe, hie ist ein lar vas, das bedarff wol, das man es fülle, mein Herr, fülle es, ich bin schwach im glauben, stercke mich, ich bin kaldt in der liebe, werme mich unnd mache mich hitzig, das meine liebe herausser fliesse auff meinen nechsten, ich hab nicht ein festen, starcken glauben, ich zweyfel zu zeyten unnd kan Gott nicht gentzlich vertrawen, Ach Herre, hilff mir, mere mir meinen glauben und vertrawen, Yn dich hab ich den schatz aller meiner gutter verschlossen, ich bin arm. Du bist [. . .] reich und bist kommen sich der armen zu erbarmen, ich bin ehn sünder und du bist gerecht, Hie bei mir ist der flus der sünde, yn dir aber ist alle fülle und gerechtigkait. . . . den wil ich haben, von welchem ich nemen kan, nicht dem ich geben darff.

67. Prayer for Perseverance in Holiness
Martin Luther (1483–1546) ❧ *26*

Ach mein lieber her Jesu criste, dw erkennest mein arme sele, und meynen grossen gebrechen, den ich dir allein mit offenem herczen klage.

Ich befinde leider, das ich nicht habe einen solchen willen und vorsacz, als ich yhn wol solt haben, und fall teglich dohin als ein kranckes sundiges mensch, und dw weist, das ich yhe gerne, einen solchen willen und vorsacz wolthe haben, und mich doch mein feindt yhm stricke fuhret gefangen, Erloße mich armen sunder nach deinem götlichen willen von allem ubel und anfechtungen, Stercke und vormehre yn mir den wahren rechten cristlichen glauben, gib mir gnade meynen nehsten aus gancz meynem herczen, getrewlichn und als mich selbst, brüderlichn zw belibenn, Borleihe mir geduldt yn verfolgunge, und aller widderwertickeit, Dw hast yhe Zw sancto petro gesagtt, das er nicht alleine sieben mahl vorgeben solt, und uns heissen tröstlichen von dir bitten, So kohme ich yn zwuorsicht solchs deines zusagens und gepietens, und klage dir als meynem rechtn pfarer und Bischoffe meyner seelen, all meyne nott. Dan dw allein weist, wie und wehn mir Zw helffen ist[.] Dein wille der geschehe und sen gebenedeiett ewiglich[.] A.m.e.n.

68. Prayer for Repentance
Martin Bucer (1491–1555) ❧ *27*

Oh Lord God and heauenly Father, which art a iust Iudge to punishe all them, that do contynewe to offende the, as thou art a Father most pytyfull to receaue to mercy all those, whiche geue ouer themselues to please the, shewe me thy grace and fauour, so that I may be truly touchid withe inward displeasure of my synnes, and that in the place of flattering my self to slepe in synne, I may be so cast downe in hart, that the rather I may truly with mouthe confesse most humbly to geue the, the honour, glory, and prayse, dew vnto thy holy name, and that as thou of thy greate mercy doste instruct vs therevnto by thy holy word, so (for thy names sake) make that ye same may so lighten and cleare our conscience, that in dew examination of all our hole lyffe, we may truly learne to be angry & displeasid with all our former, and corrupte lyuing. Oh that it may please the to drawe nere vnto vs, in addressyng and guydyng our footsteppes in the true and perfect way of obedyence to thy holy lawes and cōmaundementes. Send thy holye Angel to nitche his tentes round about vs, that his infernall army, neuer preuayle against vs, but allways with strong faith we may thorough Iesus Christ withstand all his crafty engins and snares, knowynge vndoubtedly that thou neuer forsakest them that put their trust in the. Oh let vs not be led by the infirmytie of our vntowarde fleshe, but strenghten vs by the vertue of the holy spiryte. Suffer vs not to lye vnder thy heuy wrathe & vengeaunce throughe Ipocrysye, but rather touche vs so inwardly, that we may without ceasyng, syghe, and grone vnto the, by true and vnfayned repentaunce. And althoughe we be not allwayes so wel disposyd to aske & praye, as we ought to do, yet (good Lord) for thy names sake, stretche out thy mightie hande, that by the gratious workyng of thy holy Spirite, our myndes and hartes may be drawen from all erthly and corruptible thinges, so that our prayers may procede of an ernest and inward affection, so that we neuer presume to cōme before y^t with a dobell hart, knowing that whosoeuer askethe and prayeth for anye thing of the, not asking in faith, can not obteyne. Increace our faithe therfore (oh mercyfull Father) that we presently may lyue ly the benefit of remission and pardon of all our synnes, thoroughe the merytes and death of Christ Iesus our Sauiour, and so work in vs foreuer hereafter to lyue in thy feare, and to stand in awe of thy displeasure, that thou mayst contynew our mercyfull Father world without end. God graunt yt.

69. Prayer for Divine Defense

Thomas Cranmer (1489–1556) ❧ *28*

Almyghtye God, geve us grace, that we may cast awaye the workes of darkenes, and put upon us the armour of light, now in the tyme of this mortall lyfe, (in the whiche thy sonne Jesus Christe came to visite us in great humilitie;) that in the last daye when he shal come again in his glorious majestye to judge bothe the quicke and the dead, we maye ryse to the lyfe immortal, through him who liveth and reigneth with thee and the holy ghoste now and ever. Amen.

70. Prayer for the Reading of Scripture
Thomas Cranmer (1489–1556) ❧ *28*

Blessed lord, which hast caused all holy Scriptures to bee written for our learnyng; graunte us that we maye in suche wise heare them, read, marke, learne, and inwardly digeste them; that by pacience, and coumfort of thy holy woorde, we may embrace, and ever holde fast the blessed hope of everlasting life, which thou hast geven us in our saviour Jesus Christe.

73. Prayer for Unity in the Faith
John Calvin (1509–1564) ❧ *29*

Grant, Almighty God, that since, at the coming of Christ thy Son, thou didst really perform what thy servants, the Prophets, had previously so much foretold, and since thou daily invitest us to the unity of faith, that with united efforts we may truly serve thee,—O grant, that we may not continue torn asunder, every one pursuing his own perverse inclinations, at a time when Christ is gathering us to thee; nor let us only profess with the mouth and in words, that we are under thy government, but prove that we thus feel in real sincerity: and may we then add to the true and lawful worship of thy name brotherly love towards one another, that with united efforts we may promote each other's good, and that our adoption may thus be proved and be more and more confirmed, that we may ever be able with full confidence to call on thee as our Father, through Christ our Lord. Amen.

74. Prayer for Christian Growth
John Calvin (1509–1564) ❧ *29*

Grant, Almighty God, since we have already entered in hope upon the threshold of our eternal inheritance, and know that there is a mansion for us in heaven since Christ, our head and the first fruits of our salvation, has been received there, grant that we may proceed more and more in the way of thy holy calling until at length we reach the goal, and so enjoy that eternal glory of which thou givest us a taste in this world by the same Christ, our Lord. Amen.

75. Prayer for a Quiet Mind
Henry Bull (d. ca. 1575) ❧ *30*

There is nothing (O Lord) more like to thy holie nature, then a quiet mind. Thou hast called vs out of the troublesome disquietnesse of the world, into that thy quiet rest and peace, which the world can not giue, being such a peace as passeth all mens vnderstanding. Houses are ordained for vs, that thereby we might be defended from the iniurie of the wether, from crueltie of beastes, from disquietnesse of people, and rest from the toyles of the world. O gratious father, graunt that through thy great mercy my body may enter into this house, from outward actions, but so, that it may become boxom and obedient to the soule, and make no resistaunce againste the same, that in soule and body I may haue a godly quietnesse and peace to praise thy holie name. Amen.

76. Prayer for Divine Assistance
Henry Bull (d. ca. 1575) ✹ *30*

Thou knowest Lord, what is most profitable & expedient for mee: wherfore doe with mee in all things as it shall seeme best vnto thee. For it may not bee but well that thou dost, which doest moste iustly & blessedly dispose all thinges after thy most godly wisedome. Therefore whether it be by prosperitie or aduersitie, losse or gaine, sickenesse or health, life or death, thy will be done.

Cast out of my heart, all vnprofitable cares of worldly thinges, and suffer mee not to be led with the vnstable desires of earthly vanities: but giue me grace that all worldly and carnall affections may be mortified & die in me.

Graunt vnto mee the strength of thy holy spirite, to sub-due this body of sinne with the whole lustes thereof, that it may bee obedient both in will, minde and members, to doe thy holy will.

Assist me with thy grace (O Lord) that I may be strengthened in the inwarde man, and be armed with thy holy armour, whiche is the brestplace of righteousnes, the shielde of of faith, the hope of saluation for an helmet, and the sworde of the spirite, which is thy holy word, that I may stand perfect in all that is thy will and bee found worthie, through, Christ, to receiue the crowne of life which thou hast promised to all them that loue thee.

Giue me grace that I may esteme all thinges in this world as they be, transitory & soone vanishing away, and my self also with them drawing towardes mine ende: For nothinge vnder the sunne maye longe abide, but all is vanitie and affliction of spirite.

77. Prayer for God's Grace
Lancelot Andrewes (1555–1626) ✷ *31*

Grant me O Lord thy grace.
To remember the latter end, Deut. 32. 29.
To bruise the Serpents head, Gen. 3. 15.
To cut off occasions of sinne.
To covenant with my sence, 2 Cor. 11. 13.
To prevent scandals Iob. 31. 1.

To subdue my body. Ez. 14. 4.

Not to sit idle. 1 Cor. 9. 8.

To shun wicked company. Mat. 24. 6.

To consort with the righteous. Psal. 26. 4.

To select times for prayer. 1 Cor. 7. 5.

Stopp up my pathes with thornes that I finde not the
way to vanity. Hos. 2. 6.

Hold me in and rayne me with bitt and bridle, when
I keep not neer thee. Psal. 32. 9.

And constraine mee to come to thee, If inviting will not
serve. Luc. 14. 34. 39.

78. Prayer for Deliverance

Lancelot Andrewes (1555–1626) ✍ *31*

From all Innovations, private interpretations difference
in doctrine, contending about vaine and fruitles
questions; endles desputations, and controversies.

Heresies both publique and private.

Schismes

Scandalls

From the pernicious flattering of Princes. Acts. 12. 22.

The partiality of Saul. 1 Sam. 14. 18.

The contempt of Michal. 2 Sam. 6. 16.

The Preisthood of Micha. Judg. 17. 10.

The flesh-hook of Hophni. 1 Sam. 2. 16.

The fraternity of Symon Magus, and Judas Iscariot. Act.
    8. 17. Mat. 26. 17.

From such as are corrupted in minde, unstable and
    unlearned. 1 Tim. 6. 5. 2 Pet. 3. 16.

From the arrogance of young Schollers. 1 Tim. 36.

And from People that contradict their Minister, speaking
    according to the word of God, Be mercifull good
    Lord and deliver us. Hos. 4. 4.

79. Prayer for Stewarding Wealth

George Webbe (1581–1642) ❧ *32*

O Lord God, who art infinite in greatnesse, power, glory,
and Maiesty: for all that is in the Heauen, and in the earth,
is thine; thine is the Kingdome, O Lord, and thou art exalted
ouer all: Both Riches and Honour come of thee: in thine
hand is power and might: In thine hand it is to make great,
and to giue strength to all; blessed be thy holy name, as for
all thy mercies which from time to time thou hast vouchsafed
to mee thy most unworthy Seruant; so in particular, for
that large and ample portion of these thine earthly blessings
which thou hast giuen me aboue many other of thy seruants,
whereby I might bee the better enable to serue thee, and
to set forth thy glory. For what am I? Or what is there in

mee? That thine hand hath beene so bountifull unto mee? I acknowledge that it was not any desert of mine, neither was it my labor, wit, or industry, that haue procured this wealth and riches about me, but thine onely fauour and mercy towards me. Now therefore, O my God, I thanke thee, and praise thy glorious name for this my store: Humbly beseeching thy diuine Maiesty, that thine inward blessing may accompany these thine outward blessings. Sanctifie them, good Lord, unto me, and me unto thy selfe, that I may use these blessings of thine aright, and may be found a faithfull Steward of that which thou hast comitted to my charge. Assist me with thy grace, that I may not ouer-value this wealth aboue it's worth; let not my heart be set upon it, neither let it withdraw my heart from thee. Preserue and keepe mee from pride, securitie, unthankefulnesse, couetousnesse, greedinesse, slothfulnesse, and negligence in the duties of thy seruice, together with all other temptations, snares and foolish lusts, which commonly doe accompany worldly wealth, and riches. Let not my prosperity puffe me up, nor choak the seed of thy Word, nor impouerish spiritual graces in me: Let them not infatuate mine understanding, nor make me blinde in the way to Heauen; let them not breed in me impenitencie, and hardnesse of heart, nor expose mee to thy heauy wrath and iudgements. Deliver me from the many cares, feares, sorrowes, and manifold dangers, which accompany Riches. And forasmuch as by the addition of these temporal things thou hast vouchsafed mee a double portion: So, good Lord, assist me with thy grace, that I may redouble my dutiful diligence in thy seruice. Giue me grace to remember that it was not my power, nor the strength of mine owne hand that hath prepared me this abundance: but thou the Lord, who hast giuen mee power to get substance. Giue mee grace euermore, and in all things to keep a good conscience. Make these thy blessings unto mee, instruments and meanes of well-doing. Let mee so use this world, as though I used it not. Giue mee that comfort in these earthly goods which thou allottest unto them that feare thee. Continue and so increase my store (if it bee thy blessed will) that I may haue enough for my Family, and may lay up somewhat for my posterity: and not onely so, but that I may haue alwaies somewhat to giue unto him that needeth. Giue me true contentment in that which thou giuest unto mee, and make me willing to leaue all my wealth and riches, whensoeuer it shall please thee to take them from me. O let me not mis-spend the wealth which thou hast giuen me, in excessive, vanity, and ryot, neither to impropriate it only to my selfe, as if it were mine owne, but as a good & faithfull Steward, employ them to the honour of thee my Master, and the good of my fellow seruants. Grant, O heavenly Father, that I may so use these things temporall, that finally I lose not things eternall.

Giue me grace euermore truely to serue, glorify, & honour thee, and to put my trust in thee the liuing God, who giuest us richly all things to enioy, that I may doe good, and bee rich in good workes, ready to distribute, willing to communicate, laying up in store for my selfe a good foundation against the time to come, that I may lay hold on eternall Life; To the which, I beseech thee to brnig [*sic*] mee, through the merits of thy deare Sonne, my blessed Sauiour Iesus Christ: To whom with thee and thine holy Spirit, bee ascribed all honour and glory, praise, power, might and dominion, now and for euermore. Amen.

80. Prayer for Open Hands
Jeremy Taylor (1613–1667) ❧ *33*

Thou hast called unto me to open my hand, and thou wouldest will it: but I would not open it; I held the world fast, and kept my hand shut, and would not let it go. But do thou open it for me; not my hand only, but my mouth; not my mouth, but my heart also. Grant that I may know nothing but thee, account all things loss in comparison of thee, and endeavour to be made conformable to thee.

81. Prayer for Intimacy with Christ
Jeremy Taylor (1613–1667) ❧ *33*

Eternal God, sweetest Jesu, who didst receive Judas with the affection of a Saviour, and sufferedst him to kiss Thy cheek, with the serenity and tranquillity of God; and didst permit the soldiers to bind Thee, with patience exemplary to all ages of martyrs; and didst cure the wound of Thy enemy, with the charity of a parent, and the tenderness of an infinite pity; O kiss me with the kisses of Thy mouth, embrace me with the entertainments of a gracious Lord, and let my soul dwell and feast in Thee, who art the repository of eternal sweetness and refreshments. Bind me, O Lord, with those bands which tied Thee fast, the chains of love; that such holy union may dissolve the cords of vanity, and confine the bold pretensions of usurping passions, and imprison all extravagancies of an impertinent spirit, and lead sin captive to the dominion of grace and sanctified reason; that I also may imitate all the parts of Thy holy passion; and may, by Thy bands, get my liberty; by Thy kiss, enkindle charity; by the touch of Thy hand and the breath of Thy mouth, have all my wounds cured, and restored to the integrity of a holy penitent, and the purities of innocence; that I may love Thee, and please Thee, and live with Thee for ever, O holy and sweetest Jesu. Amen.

82. Prayer for Godly Desires
Jeremy Taylor (1613–1667) ❧ *33*

Fix my thoughts, my hopes and my desires upon Heaven and heavenly things; teach me to despise the world, to repent me deeply for my sins; give me holy purposes of amendment, and ghostly strength & assistances to perform faithfully whatsoever I shall intend piously. Enrich my understanding with an eternal treasure of Divine truths, that I may know thy will, and thou who workest in us to will and to do of thy good pleasure; teach me to obey all thy Commandments, to believe all thy Revelations, and make me partaker of all thy gracious promises.

83. Prayer for Protection from Temptations
Jeremy Taylor (1613–1667) ❧ *33*

Teach me to watch over all my wayes, that I may never be surpriz'd by sudden temptations or a carelesse spirit, nor ever return to folly and vanity. Set a watch, O Lord, before my mouth, and keep the door of my lips, that I offend in my tongue neither against piety nor charity. Teach mee to think of nothing but thee and what is in order to thy glory and service; to speak nothing but thee and thy glories; and to do nothing but what becomes thy servant whom thy infinite mercy by the graces of thy holy Spirit hath sealed up to the day of Redemption.

84. Prayer for Holy Living
Jeremy Taylor (1613–1667) ❧ *33*

Let no riches ever make me forget my self; no poverty ever make me to forget thee: Let no hope or fear, no pleasure or pain, no accident without, no weaknesse within, hinder or discompose my duty, or turn me from the wayes of thy Commandements. O let thy Spirit dwell with me for ever, and make my soul just and charitable, full of honesty, full of religion, resolute and constant in holy purposes, but inflexible to evil. Make me humble and obedient, peaceable and pious; let me never envy any mans good, nor deserve to be despised my self; and if I be, teach me to bear it with meeknesse and charity.

85. Prayer for Marriage
Jeremy Taylor (1613–1667) ❧ *33*

O Eternal and gracious Father who hast consecrated the holy estate of marriage to become mysterious, and to represent the union of Christ and his Church, let thy holy Spirit so guide me in the doing the duties of this state, that it may not become a sin unto me; nor that liberty which thou hast hallowed by the holy Jesus, become an occasion of licentiousnesse by my own weakenesse and sensuality: and do thou forgive all those irregularities and too sensual applications which may have in any degree discomposed my spirit and the severity of a Christian. Let me in all accidents and circumstances be severe in my duty towards thee, affectionate and dear to my wife [or Husband] a guide and good example to my family, and in all quietnesse, sobriety, prudence and peace a follower of those holy pairs who have served thee with godlinesse and a good testimony: and the blessings of the eternal God, blessings of the right hand, and of the left be upon the body and soul of thy servant my Wife [or Husband] and abide upon her [or him] till the end of a holy and happy life; and grant that both of us may live together for ever in the embraces of the holy and eternal Jesus, our Lord and Saviour. Amen.

86. Prayer for Help during Temptations
Jeremy Taylor (1613–1667) ✎ *33*

O Lord God of infinite mercy, of infinite excellency, who hast sent thy holy Son into the world to redeem us from an intolerable misery, and to teach us a holy religion, and to forgive us an infinite debt: give me thy holy Spirit, that my understanding and all my faculties may be so resigned to the discipline and doctrine of my Lord, that I may be prepared in minde and will to dye for the testimony of Jesus, and to suffer any affliction or calamity that shall offer to hinder my duty, or tempt me to shame or sin, or apostacy: and let my faith be the parent of a good life, a strong shield to repell the fiery darts of the Devil, and the Author of a holy hope, of modest desires, of confidence in God, and of a never failing charity to thee my God, and to all the world, that I may never have my portion with the unbelievers, or uncharitable, and desperate persons; but may be supported by the strengths of faith in all temptations, and may be refreshed with the comforts of a holy hope in all my sorrows, and may bear the burden of the Lord, and the infirmities of my neighbour by the support of charity, that the yoak of Jesus may become easy to me, and my love may do all the miracles of grace, till from grace it swell to glory, from earth to heaven, from duty to reward, from the imperfections of a beginning, and little growing love it may arrive to the consummation of an eternal and never ceasing charity, through Jesus Christ the Son of thy love, the Anchor of our hope, and the Author and finisher of our faith, to whom with thee, O Lord God, Father of Heaven and Earth, and with thy holy Spirit be all glory, and love, and obedience, and dominion now and for ever. Amen.

87. Prayer for Divine Pity

Jeremy Taylor (1613–1667) ❧ *33*

O Eternal God, Father of Mercyes and God of all comfort with much mercy look upon the sadnesses and sorrowes of thy servant. My sins lye heavy upon me, and presse me sore, and there is no health in my bones by reason of thy displeasure and my sin. The waters are gone over me, and I stick fast in the deep mire, and my miseries are without comfort, because they are punishments of my sin: and I am so evil and unworthy a person, that though I have great desires, yet I have no dispositions or worthiness towards receiving comfort. My sins have caused my sorrow, and my sorrow does not cure my sins: and unless for thy own sake, and merely because thou art good, thou shalt pity me & relieve me, I am as much without remedy, as now I am without comfort. Lord pity me; Lord let thy grace refresh my Spirit. Let thy comforts support me, thy mercy pardon me, and never let my portion be amongst hopelesse and accursed spirits; for thou art good and gracious; and I throw my self upon thy mercy. Let me never let my hold go, & do thou with me what seems good in thy own eyes: I cannot suffer more then I have deserved: and yet I can need no relief so great as thy mercy is: for thou art infinitely more merciful then I can be miserable: and thy mercy which is above all thy own works, must needs be far above all my sin and all my misery. Dearest Jesus, let me trust in thee for ever, and let me never be confounded. *Amen.*

88. Prayer for Christian Unity
Jeremy Taylor (1613–1667) ❧ *33*

O holy Jesus King of the Saints, and Prince of the Catholick Church, preserve thy spouse whom thou hast purchased with thy right hand, and redeemed and cleansed with thy blood; the whole Catholick Church from one end of the Earth to the other; she is founded upon a rock, but planted in the sea. O preserve her safe from schisme, heresy, and sacriledge. Unite all her members with the bands of Faith, Hope and Charity, and an external communion, when it shall seem good in thine eyes: let the daily sacrifice of prayer and Sacramental thanksgiving never cease, but be for ever presented to thee, and for ever united to the intercession of her dearest Lord, and for ever prevail for the obtaining for every of its members grace and blessing, pardon and salvation. *Amen.*

89. Prayer for Sanctification
Henry Scougal (1650–1678) ❧ *34*

O most gracious God, Father and Fountain of Mercy and Goodness, who hast blessed us with the Knowledge of our

Happiness, and the way that leadeth unto it, excite in our Souls such ardent desires after the one, as may put us forth to the diligent prosecution of the other: Let us neither presume of our own strength, nor distrust thy Divine Assistance; but while we are doing our utmost endeavours, teach us still to depend on Thee for the success. Open our Eyes, O God, and teach us out of thy Law: Bless us with an exact and tender sense of our duty, and a taste to discern perverse things: O that our wayes were directed to keep thy Statutes, then shall we not be ashamed when we have respect unto all thy Commandments: Possess our hearts with a generous and holy disdain of all those poor enjoyments which this World holdeth out to allure us, that they may never be able to inveigle our Affections, or betray us unto any Sin: Turn away our eyes from beholding vanity, and quicken thou us in thy Law. Fill our Souls with such a deep sense and full perswasion of those great Truths which Thou hast reveal'd in the Gospel, as may influence and regulate our whole Conversation, and that the life which we henceforth live in the flesh, we may live through Faith in the Son of God. O that the infinite Perfections of thy Blessed Nature, and the astonishing Expressions of thy Goodness and Love, may conquer and overpower our hearts, that they may be constantly arising towards Thee in flames of Devoutest Affection, and inlarging themselves in Sincere and Cordial Love towards all the World for thy sake: and that we may cleanse our selves from all filthiness of the flesh and spirit, perfecting holiness in thy fear, without which we can never hope to behold and enjoy Thee. Finally, O God, grant that the consideration of what thou art, and what we our selves are, may both humble and lay us low before Thee, and also stir up in us the strongest and most ardent aspirations towards Thee. We desire to resign and give up our selves to the Conduct of thy Holy Spirit: lead us in thy Truth and teach us, for thou art the God of our Salvation: Guide us with thy Counsel, and afterwards receive us unto Glory: for the Merits and Intercession of thy Blessed Son our Saviour. Amen.

90. Prayer for Divine Protection of the Heart
John Kettlewell (1653–1695) ✎ 35

I give my Heart to thee, and humbly pray, that it may always be in thy hands, since it is so unconstant in what is good, and prone to turn aside to what is evil, when it is in mine own keeping. O! Father, keep it stedfast, and unalterable in thy ways. Let it not be inclined to any Evil thing, nor lean towards any of my former Vanitys. Keep mine Eyes, from beholding wickedness; and mine Ears from listening thereto. Let not my Lips utter any thing that is Ill, nor my feet move a step in any of the Paths of Death. But hold my whole Spirit,

Soul, and Body, in ways of thy Fear; and continue me under the Comfortable hopes of thy favour, through Jesus Christ my Blessed Lord and only Saviour, Amen.

91. Prayer for Divine Peace

John Kettlewell (1653–1695) ❧ 35

Let me have thy Peace, O! Gracious Father, and comfort my trembling and broken Heart with the Hopes thereof. Cause me to hear the Voice of Joy and Gladness, and revive me with the Assurance of thy Love. O! that I may be able from my own Experience, to speak great things of thy readiness, to receive and comfort returning Sinners; and thereby draw back others to thy Service, who are still running astray from the same. O! that by seeing thy Goodness upon me, every one that is Godly may seek to thee in their Distress, and find Mercy, as I have done. But Lord, having found thy Mercy to poor Sinners, let me not abuse it, or presume upon it. Let me not take Heart to repeat my Sins, because thou art ready and glad to grant Forgiveness. When thou hast spoke comfortably to me make me carefull to sin no more lest a worse thing come upon me; but to keep on in all holy and thankful Obedience unto thee, and never more to return to folly. Let the Sence of thy Mercies, O! My God, serve no other use in me, but to encourage my

Repentance, and to support me in thy Fear, till I come at length to enjoy thy Eternal Favour, through Jesus Christ my Lord, Amen.

92. Prayer for the Morning
Isaac Watts (1674–1748) ❧ *36*
[Invocation]

Oh Lord God most high and most holy, the Creator, the Governor and the Judge of all mankind.

[Adoration]

I adore thy Majesty, and worship thee with humble reverence: Thou art infinitely wise, powerful and gracious, far beyond our highest thoughts, and above all our praises. Thou hast made the day-light for the businesses of life, and hast raised me from the bed of sleep to see another morning with Comfort.

[Confession]

I acknowledge before thee I am utterly unworthy to come into thy holy presence: My original is from the dust, and my iniquities have render'd me viler than the beasts that perish. I am by nature unholy and unclean: and tho' my years are but few, yet my sins are many: my daily actual transgressions witness against me, and deserve destruction from the hand of thy justice, so that I can make no pretence to merit before thy throne: But there is forgiveness with thee, that sinners may be encouraged to return to thee with hope and love.

[Petitions for one's self.]

[1.] Let thy mercy, O Lord, blot out all my offences, for the sake of the sufferings of thy beloved Son, and let a sinful creature find favour in thy sight, upon the account of his complete Obedience, and his bloody death.

[2] Pity me, O heavenly Father, under my natural blindness and ignorance. Instruct me by thy word and thy good Spirit, that I may know more of my self, and my own wants and weaknesses, and that I may know thee better in the discoveres of thy grace. Teach me the precepts of thy law, that I may learn what is my duty, and let me grow daily into a humble acquaintance with Christ Jesus, who is the righteousness and the strength and the life of his people.

[3] Work in my heart sincere repentance for all my past offenses, and let my faith in Jesus be such as thou wilt approve, such as may draw my heart near to God in holy love, and produce the good fruits of obedience in the whole course of my life. I would commit my self into his hands, as my only and my all-sufficient Saviour, to deliver me both from sin and from hell, and to bring me safe to his heavenly kingdom.

[4] Form my soul, O Lord, after thy holy Image, which was lost by the sin of my first Parents. Rectify all the irregular inclinations that are within me. Keep me from the power of unruly appetites, and from sudden and ungovernable passions of every kind. Help me to set a constant watch over all my senses, and the wandering imaginations of my heart. Suppress all undue resentments of whatsoever injuries I meet with: Let such a meek and serene temper be wrought in me, as appeared in my blessed Saviour here on earth, for I would fain be like him, and imitate his holy pattern. Kindle in my soul such a pious flame of love to God, and charity towards men, that I may make it my delight to do good to all, even to those who have done me hurt. But let my love in a special manner go out towards all those who bear thine Image, and who love Jesus thy Son, whatsoever lesser differences of party, opinion or interest may be between us. . . .

[7] When thou feelstt needful to correct me, O my God, let it be done in measure and in mercy, and let the fruit and effect thereof be to take away my sins, and make me partaker of thy holiness.

[Resignation]

I resign my self up entirely to they good pleasure, and to the conduct of thy wisdom, according to the covenant of thy grace. I desire to be thine in life and death, and in the world to come for ever.

[Petitions for others]

[1] Nor would I pray for my self only, but for all men, as thou hast taught me. Enlighten the whole earth with the light of thy Gospel: Deliver those that are persecuted for Righteousness sake, from the hands of those that hate them, and let the spirit of persecution be rooted out from among men: When shall the time come, O Lord, that the liberties of mankind, and of thy Gospel shall be asserted and vindicated by the Rules of this world? When shall it be that the Kings of all the earth shall bring their power and glory to support the cause of true Religion? . . .

[4] Maintain thy Gospel in its power and glory: Let the ministry of thy word be attended with a publick supply of thy Spirit, that thy Church on earth may be enlarged daily, and knowledge and holiness may increase and abound among men.

[5]. Look down in mercy on my dear Relations and Friends. Bless my Parents and Kindred with all necessary gifts of Providence and of Grace. Manifest thy love to all those that love me, and enable me from my heart to forgive all that have done me hurt: Let them repent of their sins, O Lord, and be made partakers of thy forgiveness. . . .

[Thanksgiving]

In his name also would I offer up my humble thanks for all the mercies I enjoy, and for all that I hope for. It is to thee, O God, that I owe my very life and being, my health and ease, and the use of my senses and my limbs: Thou givest me safety in the night, and the blessings of the morning. It is from thee I derive all the benefits of food and rayment, the supports of nature, together with the rich promises of Grace and eternal Salvation. To thee therefore, O Lord, I pay all honour and praise.

[Blessing or Doxology]

And may the name of God my Father, my Savior and my Sanctifier, be glorified to everlasting Ages. Amen.

93. Prayer from a Heart Broken by Grief

Samuel Johnson (1709–1784) ✹ *37*

Almighty and most merciful Father, who seest all our miseries, and knowest all our necessities, look down upon me, and pity me. Defend me from the violent incursions of evil thoughts, and enable me to form and keep such resolutions as may conduce to the discharge of the duties which thy providence shall appoint me; and so help me, by thy Holy Spirit, that my heart may surely there be fixed where true joys are to be found, and that I may serve Thee with pure affection and a cheerful mind. Have mercy upon me, O God, have mercy upon me; years and infirmities oppress me, terror and anxiety beset me. Have mercy upon me, my Creator and my Judge. In all dangers protect me, in all perplexity relieve and free me, and so help me by thy Holy Spirit, that I may now so commemorate the death of thy Son our Saviour Jesus Christ, as that when this short and painful life shall have an end, I may, for his sake, be received to everlasting happiness. Amen.

94. Prayer in the Evening

John Wesley (1703–1791) ❧ *38*

Almighty and most merciful Father, in whom we live, move and have our Being; to whose tender Compassions we owe our Safety the Day past, together with all the Comforts of this Life, and the Hoeps of that which is to come. We praise Thee, O Lord, we bow ourselves before Thee, acknowledging we have nothing but what we receive from Thee. *Unto Thee do we give Thanks*, O God, who daily pourest thy Benefits upon us.

Blessed be thy Goodness for our Health, for our Food and Raiment, for our Peace and Safety, for the Love of our Friends, for all our Blessings in this Life; and our Desire to attain that Life which is immortal. Blessed be thy Love, for that we feel in our Hearts any Motion towards Thee. Behold,

O Lord, we present ourselves before Thee, to be inspired with such a vigorous Sense of thy Love, as may put us forward with the greater Earnestness, Zeal and Diligence in all our Duty. Renew in us we beseech, a lively Image of Thee, in all Righteousness, Purity, Mercy, Faithfulness and Truth. O that Jesus, the Hope of Glory, may be formed in us, in all Humility, Meekness, Patience, and an absolute Surrender of our Souls and Bodies to thy holy Will: That *we may not live, but Christ may live in us;* that every one of us may say, *The Life I now live in the Flesh, I live by Faith in the Son of God, who loved me, and gave himself for me.*

Let the Rememberance of his Love, who made himself an Offering for our Sins, be ever dear and precious to us. Let it continually move us to offer up ourselves to Thee, to do thy Will, as our blessed Master did. May we place an entire Confidence in Thee, and still trust ourselves with Thee, who hast not spared, *thine own Son, but freely given him up for us all.* May we humbly accept of whatsoever Thou sendest us, and in *every thing give Thanks.* Surely Thou *wilt never leave us nor forsake us.* O guide us safe thro' all the Changes of this Life, in an unchangeable Love to Thee, and a lively Sense of thy Love to us, 'till we come to live with Thee and enjoy Thee for ever.

And now that we are going to lay ourselves down to sleep, take us into thy gracious Protection, and settle our Spirit in such quiet and delightful Thought of the Glory where our Lord Jesus lives, that we may desire to be dissolved and go to him who died for us, that whether we wake or sleep, we should live together with him.

To thy Blessing we recommend all Mankind, high and low, rich and poor, that they may all faithfully serve Thee, and contentedly enjoy whatsoever is needful for them. And especially, we beseech Thee, that the Course of this World may be so peaceably ordered by the Governance that thy Church may joyfully serve Thee in all godly Quietness. We leave all we have with Thee, especially our Friends, and those who are dear to us desiring that when we are dead and gone, they may lift up their Souls in this Manner unto Thee; and teach those that come after, to praise, love and obey Thee. And if we awake again in the Morning, may we praise Thee again with joyful Lips, and still offer ourselves a more acceptable Sacrifice to Thee, thro' Jesus Christ, in whose Words we beseech Thee to hear us, according to the full Sense and Meaning thereof.

95. Prayer for Right Perspective
William Jay (1769–1853) ❧ *39*

O Lord, we would remember, that gratitude becomes us much more than complaint. Our afflictions have been light, compared with our guilt; and few, compared with the sufferings of others. They have all been attended with numberless alleviations: they have all been needful: all founded in a regard to our welfare: all designed to work together for our good. We bless Thee for what is past, and trust Thee for what is to come: and cast all our care upon Thee, knowing that Thou carest for us.

96. Prayer for God's Guidance
William Jay (1769–1853) ❧ *39*

O thou God of all grace; the Father of mercies, the hope of Israel, the Saviour thereof in the time of trouble: why has Thou revealed Thyself in such lovely characters, and endearing relations, but to meet our dejections, to remove our fears, and induce us to say, it is good for me to draw nigh to God.

We come to Thee as criminals to be pardoned, as beggars to obtain relief, and as friends to enjoy communion with the God of love. We bow with submission and gratitude, to the method which Thou hast appointed and made known for all intercourse between Thee and us. We approach Thee, through him in whom Thou hast proclaimed Thyself well pleased, pleading the propitiation of his blood, and making mention of his righteousness, and of his only. . . .

What we know not, teach Thou us. Lead us into all truth. May we see divine things in a divine light, that while they inform our judgment they may sanctify the heart, and consecrate the whole life to the service and glory of God. Who can understand his errors? Cleanse Thou us from secret faults. Search us, O God, and know our hearts, try us and know our thoughts, and see if there be any wicked way in us, and lead us in the way everlasting.

Accept of our united thanksgiving for the preservation and refreshment of the past night; and take us under thy guiding and guardian care this day; and whether we eat or drink, or whatever we do, may we do all to the glory of God, through our Lord and Saviour. Amen.

97. Prayer for Growing Faith
William Jay (1769–1853) ✒ *39*

Thou art the Author of all existence, and the source of all blessedness. We adore Thee for making us capable of knowing Thee; for possessing us with reason, and conscience; and for leading us to inquire where is God my Maker that giveth songs in the night. We praise Thee for all the information with which we are favoured, to bring us to thyself; especially the revelation of the gospel. Here we look into thy very heart, and see that it is the dwelling place of pity. Here we see thy thoughts towards us, and find that they are thoughts of peace and not of evil. Here we see Thee waiting to be gracious, and exalted to have mercy. Here Thou hast told our consciences how the guilty can be pardoned, the unholy can be sanctified, and the poor furnished with unsearchable riches.

May we be found in the number of those who not only hear, but know the joyful sound, that we may walk in the light of thy countenance, in thy name rejoice all the day, and in thy righteousness be exalted. May we take Thee, the God of truth, at thy word; and believe the record, that Thou hast given to us eternal life, and that this life is in thy Son. And since it is not only a faithful saying but worthy of all acceptance, that He came into the world to save sinners, to Him may we look alone for salvation, and with all the earnestness, the infinite importance of the case requires.

98. Prayer for God's Presence and Closeness
Charles Spurgeon (1834–1892) ❧ *40*

O thou who art King of kings and Lord of lords, we worship Thee.

Before Jehovah's awful throne
We bow with sacred joy.[1]

---

1 Isaac Watts, "Before Jehovah's Awful Throne" (1705).

We can truly say that we delight in God. There was a time when we feared Thee, O God, with the fear of bondage. Now we reverence, but we love as much as we reverence. The thought of Thine Omnipresence was once horrible to us. We said: "Whither shall we flee from His presence?" and it seemed to make hell itself more dreadful, because we heard a voice, "If I make my bed in hell, behold, Thou art there." But now, O Lord, we desire to find Thee. Our longing is to feel Thy presence, and it is the heaven of heavens that Thou art there. The sick bed is soft when Thou art there. The furnace of affliction grows cool when Thou art there, and the house of prayer when Thou art present is none other than the house of God, and it is the very gate of heaven.

Come near, our Father, come very near to Thy children. Some of us are very weak in body and faint in heart. Soon, O God, lay Thy right hand upon us and say unto us, "Fear not." Peradventure, some of us are alike, and the world is attracting us. Come near to kill the influence of the world with Thy superior power.

Even to worship may not seem easy to some. The dragon seems to pursue them, and floods out of his mouth wash away their devotion. Give to them great wings as of an eagle, that each one may fly away into the place prepared for him, and rest in the presence of God to-day.

Our Father, come and rest Thy children now. Take the helmet from our brow, remove from us the weight of our heavy armour for awhile, and may we just have peace, perfect peace, and be at rest. Oh! help us, we pray Thee, now. As Thou hast already washed Thy people in the fountain filled with blood and they are clean, now this morning wash us from defilement in the water. With the basin and with the ewer, O Master, wash our feet again. It will greatly refresh; it will prepare us for innermost fellowship with Thyself. So did the priests wash ere they went into the holy place.

Lord Jesus, take from us now everything that would hinder the closest communion with God. Any wish or desire that might hamper us in prayer remove, we pray Thee. Any memory of either sorrow or care that might hinder the fixing of our affection wholly on our God, take it away now. What have we to do with idols any more? Thou hast seen and observed us. Thou knowest where the difficulty lies. Help us against it, and may we now come boldly, not into the Holy place alone, but into the Holiest of all, where we should not dare to come if our great Lord had not rent the veil, sprinkled the mercy seat with His own blood, and bidden us enter.

Now, we have come close up to Thyself, to the light that shineth between the wings of the Cherubim, and we speak with Thee now as a man speaketh with his friends. Our God, we are Thine. Thou art ours. We are now concerned in one business, we are leagued together for one battle. Thy battle is our battle, and our fight is Thine. Help us, we pray Thee. Thou who didst strengthen Michael and his angels to cast out the dragon and his angels, help poor flesh and blood that to us also the word may be fulfilled: "The Lord shall bruise Satan under your feet, shortly."

Our Father, we are very weak. Worst of all we are very wicked if left to ourselves, and we soon fall a prey to the enemy. Therefore help us. We confess that sometimes in prayer when we are nearest to Thee at that very time some evil thought comes in, some wicked desire. Oh! what poor simpletons we are. Lord help us. We feel as if we would now come closer to Thee still, and hide under the shadow of Thy wings. We wish to be lost in God. We pray that Thou mayest live in us, and not we live, but Christ live in us and show Himself in us and through us.

Lord sanctify us. Oh! that Thy spirit might come and saturate every faculty, subdue every passion, and use every power of our nature for obedience to God.

Come, Holy Spirit, we do know Thee; Thou hast often overshadowed us. Come, more fully take possession of us. Standing now as we feel we are right up at the mercy seat our very highest prayer is for perfect holiness, complete consecration, entire cleansing from every evil. Take our heart, our head, our hands, our feet, and use this all for Thee. Lord take our substance, let us not hoard it for ourselves, nor spend it for ourselves. Take our talent, let us not try to educate ourselves that we may have the repute of being wise, but let every gain of mental attainment be still that we may serve Thee better.

May every breath be for Thee; may every minute be spent for Thee. Help us to live while we live and while we are busy in the world as we must be, for we are called to it, may we sanctify the world for Thy service. May we be lumps of salt in the midst of society. May our spirit and temper as well as our conversation be heavenly; may there be an influence about us that shall make the world the better before we leave it. Lord hear us in this thing.

And now that we have Thine ear we would pray for this poor world in which we live. We are often horrified by it. O, Lord, we could wish that we did not know anything about it for our own comfort. We have said, "Oh! for a lodge in some vast wilderness." We hear of oppression and robbery and murder, and men seem let loose against each other. Lord, have mercy upon this great and wicked city. What is to be done with these millions? What can we do? At least help every child of Thine to do his utmost. May none of us contribute to the evil directly or indirectly, but may we contribute to the good that is in it.

We feel we may speak with Thee now about this, for when Thy servant Abraham stood before Thee and spake with such wonderful familiarity to Thee, he pleaded for Sodom; and we plead for London. We would follow the example of the Father of the Faithful and pray for all great cities, and indeed for all the nations. Lord let Thy kingdom come. Send forth Thy light and Thy truth. Chase the old dragon from his throne, with all his hellish crew. Oh! that the day might come when even upon earth the Son of the woman, the Man-child, should rule the nations, not with a broken staff of wood, but with an enduring sceptre of iron, full of mercy, but full of power, full of grace, but yet irresistible. Oh! that that might soon come, the personal advent of our Lord! We long for the millennial triumph of His Word.

Until then, O Lord, gird us for the fight, and make us to be among those who overcome through the blood of the Lamb and through the word of our testimony, because we "love not our lives unto the death."

We lift our voice to Thee in prayer; also, for all our dear ones. Lord bless the sick and make them well as soon as it is right they should be. Sanctify to them all they have to bear.

There are also dear friends who are very weak; some that are very trembling. God bless them. While the tent is being taken down may the inhabitant within look on with calm joy, for we shall by and by "be clothed upon with our house that is from heaven." Lord help us to sit very loose by all these things here below. May we live here like strangers and make the world not a house but an inn, in which we sup and lodge, expecting to be on our journey to-morrow.

Lord save the unconverted, and bring out, we pray Thee, from among them those who are converted, but who have not confessed Christ. May the Church be built up by many who, having believed, are baptized unto the sacred name. We pray Thee go on and multiply the faithful in the land. Oh! that Thou wouldst turn the hearts of men to the gospel once more. Thy servant is often very heavy in heart because of the departures from the faith. Oh! Bring them back; let not Satan take away any more of the stars with his tail, but may the lamps of God shine bright. Oh! Thou that walkest amongst the seven golden candlesticks trim the flame, pour forth the oil, and let the light shine brightly and steadily. Now, Lord, we cannot pray any longer, though we have a thousand things to ask for. Thy servant cannot, so he begs to leave a broken prayer at the mercy seat with this at the foot of it: We ask in the name of Jesus Christ Thy Son. Amen.

99. Prayer for the Church and Society

Charles Spurgeon (1834–1892) ❧ *40*

O God! we would not speak to Thee as from a distance, nor stand like trembling Israel under the law at a distance from the burning mount, for we have not come unto Mount Sinai, but unto Mount Sion, and that is a place for holy joy and thankfulness, and not for terror and bondage. Blessed be Thy name, O Lord! We have learnt to call Thee "Our Father, which art in heaven"; so there is reverence, for Thou art in heaven; but there is sweet familiarity, for Thou art our Father.

We would draw very near to Thee now through Jesus Christ the Mediator, and we would make bold to speak to Thee as a man speaketh with his friend, for hast Thou not said by Thy Spirit, "Let us come boldly unto the throne of the heavenly grace." We might well start away and flee from Thy face if we only remembered our sinfulness. Lord! we do remember it with shame and sorrow; we are grieved to think we should have offended Thee, should have neglected so long Thy sweet love and tender mercy; but we have now returned unto the "shepherd and bishop of our souls." Led by such grace, we look to Him whom we crucified, and we have mourned for Him and then have mourned for our sin.

Now, Lord, we confess our guilt before Thee with tenderness of heart, and we pray Thee seal home to every believer here that full and free, that perfect and irreversible charter of forgiveness which Thou gavest to all them that put their trust in Jesus Christ. Lord! Thou hast said it: "If we confess our sins, Thou art merciful and just to forgive us our sins and to save us from all unrighteousness." There is the sin confessed: there is the ransom accepted: we therefore know we have peace with God, and we bless that glorious one who hath come "to finish transgression, to make an end of sin," to bring in everlasting righteousness, which righteousness by faith we take unto ourselves and Thou dost impute unto us.

Now, Lord, wilt Thou be pleased to cause all Thy children's hearts to dance within them for joy? Oh! help Thy people to come to Jesus again to-day. May we be looking unto Him to-day as we did at the first. May we never take off our eyes from His Divine person, from His infinite merit, from His finished work, from His living power, or from the expectancy of His speedy coming to "judge the world in righteousness and the people with His truth."

Bless all Thy people with some special gift, and if we might make a choice of one it would be this: "Quicken us, O Lord, according to Thy Word." We have life; give it to us more abundantly. Oh, that we might have so much life that out of the midst of us there might flow rivers of living water. The Lord make us useful. Do, dear Saviour, use the very least among us; take the one talent and let it be put out to interest for the great Father. May it please Thee to show each one of us what Thou wouldest have us to do. In our families, in our business, in the walks of ordinary life may we be serving the Lord, and may we often speak a word for His name, and help in some way to scatter the light amongst the ever-growing darkness; and ere we go hence may we have sown some seed which we shall bring with us on our shoulders in the form of sheaves of blessing.

O God! bless our Sunday schools, and give a greater interest in such work, that there may be no lack of men and women who shall be glad and happy in the work of teaching the young. Do impress this, we pray Thee, upon Thy people just now. Move men who have gifts and ability also to preach the Gospel. There are many that live in villages, and there is no gospel preaching near them. Lord! set them preaching themselves. Wilt Thou move some hearts so powerfully that their tongues cannot be quiet any longer, and may they attempt in some way, either personally or by supporting some one, to bring the gospel into dark benighted hamlets that the people may know the truth.

O Lord! stir up the dwellers in this great, great city. Oh! arouse us to the spiritual destitution of the masses. O God, help us all by some means, by any means, by every means to get at the ears of men for Christ's sake that so we may reach their hearts. We would send up an exceeding great and bitter cry to Thee on behalf of the millions that enter no place of worship, but rather violate its sanctity and despise its blessed message. Lord! wake up London, we beseech Thee. Send us another Jonah; send us another John the Baptist. Oh! that the Christ Himself would send forth multitudes of labourers amongst this thick standing corn, for the harvest truly is plenteous, but the labourers are few. Oh God! save this city; save this country; save all countries; and let Thy kingdom come; may every knee bow and confess that Jesus Christ is Lord.

Our most earnest prayers go up to heaven to Thee now for great sinners, for men and women that are polluted and depraved by the filthiest of sins. With sovereign mercy make a raid amongst them. Come and capture some of these that they may become great lovers of Him that shall forgive them, and may they become great champions for the cross.

Lord, look upon the multitudes of rich people in this city that know nothing about the gospel and do not wish to know. Oh! that somehow the poor rich might be rich with the gospel of Jesus Christ. And then, Lord, look upon the multitude of the poor and the working classes that think religion to be a perfectly unnecessary thing for them. Do, by some means we pray Thee, get them to think and bring them to listen that faith may come by hearing, and hearing by the Word of God.

Above all, O Holy Spirit, descend more mightily. Would, God, Thou wouldest flood the land till there should be streams of righteousness; for is there not a promise, "I will pour water upon him that is thirsty and floods upon the dry ground." Lord, set Thy people praying; stir up the Church to greater prayerfulness.

Now, as Thou hast bidden us, we pray for the people among whom we dwell. We pray for those in authority, for Thy benediction to all judges and rulers as also upon the poorest of the poor and the lowest of the low. Lord, bless the people; let the people praise Thee, O God! yea, let all the people praise Thee, for Jesus Christ's sake. Amen and Amen.

Historical Figure Index

Topic Index